MW01273012

An
Executive Briefing
and
Plan-to-Plan Day

STRATEGIC
AND
SYSTEMS THINKING

To accelerate your shift
to the "Systems Age"

From: Chaos & Complexity
To: Elegant Simplicity

Your Personal

Executive Briefing Booklet

and Workbook

1420 Monitor Road • San Diego • California • 92110-1545 • (619) 275-6528 • Fax (619) 275-0324

> The future has always been difficult to handle, so . . . it is really a challenge that requires a broad input. Companies and industries die because executives did not think of what is yet to come.
>
> —*Adapted from P. Crosby*
>
> **A Basic Reorientation of Our Thinking is Needed**
> In one way or another, we are forced to deal with complexities, with "wholes" or "systems" in all fields of knowledge. This implies a basic reorientation in scientific thinking.
>
> —*Ludwig van Bertalanffy*

The Centre's "Nothing to Lose" Guarantee
How to Get Started on Your Enterprise-Wide Change Process:
A "Value-Added" One Day Meeting

Dear Participant:

As a way to get started on your progression to the "Systems Age", this set of four concepts will accelerate your paradigm shift to become a Strategic and Systems Thinker. You can apply these concepts to creating Customer Value, Strategic Planning and/or all kinds of change projects. To do this properly, we recommend a one-day Executive Briefing and Plan-to-Plan Process with the Centre for Strategic Management® focused on your project. In this one day, we are able to educate each other on either 1) strategic planning, 2) creating customer value, or 3) any large scale change project you are planning to implement. It allows us to get together on the same page and address with your specific situation. We also mutually assess, analyze, decide, and tailor what type of Enterprise-Wide Change Management project, if any, should go beyond this one-day event.

We are so confident of our ability to help you during this one day immersion that we offer a "Nothing to Lose" Guarantee for this event with your top management team. If you do not receive a "Value-Added" day from the time we spend together, pay us our expenses only and the day's fee is waived.

Happy Reading,

Stephen S. Haines

Stephen G. Haines, President
San Diego, California
(619) 275-6528

P.S.   To really understand Strategic & Systems Thinking fully, please ask us about our **Product Catalogue featuring all of our support tools**.

ebsstcover.pmd

"Strategic & Systems Thinking"

From theory ➔ to practice

From complexity ➔ to simplicity

From confusing complexity ➔ to elegant simplicity

From tradition ➔ to innovation

From analytic/reductionistic thinking ➔ to systems thinking

From mechanic ➔ to organic thinking

From parts ➔ to the whole

From tactical ➔ to Strategic Thinking

Purposes:

1. To provide a brief overview of the history, research and science of General Systems Theory and the leap to the Systems Age in the 21st Century.

2. To assist participants in beginning to understand and improve their thought processes and knowledge in Strategic Thinking as applied to organizations, teams and individuals.

3. To discover, examine, and learn the four key concepts of the science of Living Systems as the natural and better way the world works.

4. To help each participant walk away with a beginning set of practical tools, tips, and techniques to actually use Systems Thinking strategically in their daily work and daily lives.

5. To plan the next steps and priorities for spreading this new strategic "orientation to life" to the rest of your organization, in a tailored way that creates a Culture of Business Excellence and Superior Results.

6. Optional alternative purpose: To assist participants in improving their thought processes, knowledge, and practical skills in Systems Thinking, as applied to going "Beyond the Learning Organization" and individuals/teams as well.

Why Learn Strategic & Systems Thinking?

Key Feature: It is a more productive language based on a **better** way to think...to act and to achieve extraordinary results. It is truly a **"new orientation to life"** once it is internalized.

Key Benefit: Ordinary People + Extraordinary Thinking = Strategic Thinking = **Extraordinary Results**...time after time.

ebsstcover.pmd

1420 Monitor Road • San Diego • California • 92110-1545 • (619) 275-6528 • Fax (619) 275-0324

STRATEGIC & SYSTEMS THINKING:
"Beyond the Learning Organization"

(CONCEPTS, LEARNINGS, & APPLICATIONS)

Table of Contents

1420 Monitor Road • San Diego • California • 92110-1545 • (619) 275-6528 • Fax (619) 275-0324

One Day Executive Briefing and Plan-to-Plan
Strategic Thinking and Learning

Agenda

8:30 **I.** **Introduction**
- Purposes, Agenda, Wants
- Logistics, To Do List, Norms
- 3 Goals and 3 Premises
- Strategic Management—Our Only Business

II. **Executive Briefing**
1. Overview—Science and the Age of Systems Thinking
2. Strategic Thinking Defined and Contrasted
3. Systems Thinking Basics
4. Hierarchy of Living Systems
5. The ABCs of Strategic Management
6. Historical Cycles of Change
7. (Optional – as time permits) Learning to Learn

12:00 **Lunch**

1:00 8. Summary of Strategic and Systems Thinking

2:00 **III.** **Plan-to-Plan Process**
1. Big 3 Enterprise-Wide Failure Issues
2. Players of Change
3. Conduct "Tailored To Your Needs" Exercise
   - Post/assess results
4. Next Steps Decided
5. Action Planning

4:30 **IV.** **Summary, Closure**

Prework
Reading the 4-page Executive Summary Article on *Systems Thinking and Learning*

Executive Briefing Materials
1. This Booklet
2. *Managers Pocket Guide to Systems Thinking and Learning*
3. Employee Handbook #2 and Plastic Job Aid/Trifold
4. 4-Color *Systems Thinking* Model/4 Concepts
5. 4-Color *Reinventing Strategic Management* Model
6. 4-Color *Business Excellence Architecture* Model

ebsstcover.pmd

1420 Monitor Road • San Diego • California • 92110-1545 • (619) 275-6528 • Fax (619) 275-0324

THE ABCs OF
STRATEGIC MANAGEMENT℠

Definition:

Strategic Planning

Plus

Strategic Change Management

Three Goals:

#1   Develop Strategic, Business, and Annual Plans and Document(s).

#2   Ensure their Successful Implementation, Innovation, and Change.

#3   Build and Sustain High Performance over the long-term.

Three Main Premises:

#1   Planning and Change Management are *the Primary* parts of Leadership and Management Roles.

#2   "People support what they help create."

#3   Use Systems Thinking. Focus on Outcomes – Serve the Customer.

Five Phases of STRATEGIC MANAGEMENT

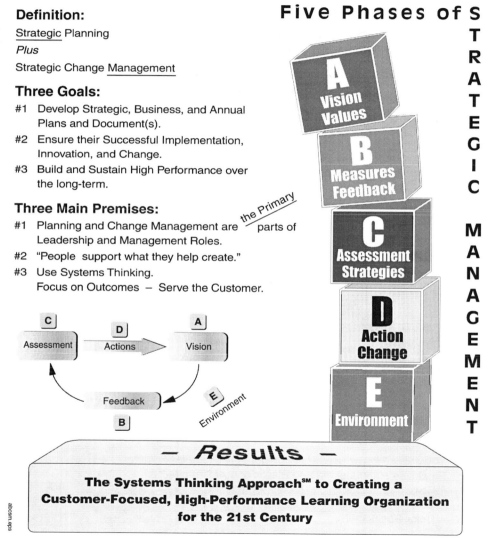

– Results –

The Systems Thinking Approach℠ to Creating a Customer-Focused, High-Performance Learning Organization for the 21st Century

abcsm.eps

ebsstcover.pmd

Page EBSST-6

1420 Monitor Road • San Diego • California • 92110-1545 • (619) 275-6528 • Fax (619) 275-0324

STRATEGIC MANAGEMENT
"Our Only Business"

"Positioning Organizations to Create Customer Value"

Strategic Edge

Creation of a Strategic Management System:

#2 Strategic Planning/Positioning
- Business Planning

#3 Enterprise-Wide Change Management

"STRATEGIC BUSINESS DESIGN"

People Edge

Attunement With People:

#4 Strategic HR Management
- Executive Coaching and Team Building

#5 Leadership and Managament Development System

Customer Edge

Alignment of Delivery:

#6 Strategic Marketing, Sales and Service

#7 Performance Excellence
- Value Chain Management
- Process Improvement

Greater Choice

Faster Response

#8 Customer Value

Better Service

Lower Cost

Higher Quality

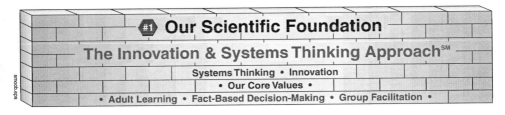

#1 **Our Scientific Foundation**

The Innovation & Systems Thinking Approach℠

Systems Thinking • Innovation
• Our Core Values •
• Adult Learning • Fact-Based Decision-Making • Group Facilitation •

smoob.eps

ebsstcover.pmd

1420 Monitor Road • San Diego • California • 92110-1545 • (619) 275-6528 • Fax (619) 275-0324

HAVE YOU EVER THOUGHT OF THIS?

- All the literature that has ever been written in the modern English language consists of patterns of only 26 letters.

- All the paintings ever made are patterns of only three primary colors.

- All the music ever written consists of patterns of no more than 12 notes.

- All the arithmetical expressions we know consist of only 10 symbols.

- And for the vast computations of digital computers, everything is made of patterns of only two components.

- Thus, whenever we speak of something as being 'new', we are really talking about original patterns of already existing components.

Source: Don Fabun, Three Roads to Awareness

1420 Monitor Road • San Diego • California • 92110-1545 • (619) 275-6528 • Fax (619) 275-0324

CRITICAL ISSUES LIST

#2.   What are the 5-10 most important critical/strategic issues facing you today as an organization?

1.

2.

3.

4.

5.

6.

7.

8.

9.

10.

If Strategic Planning is going smoothly, we're doing something wrong

(unless we have infinite resources).

Challenge the Obvious!

Note: Use this list as the content framework and "grounding" for the strategic thinking process. Bring it out at the end of the planning process to ensure you've covered these issues adequately.

ebsstcover.pmd

1420 Monitor Road • San Diego • California • 92110-1545 • (619) 275-6528 • Fax (619) 275-0324

Our Level of Thinking

Problems that are created
by our current level of thinking
can't be solved
by that same level of thinking.

—Albert Einstein

So . . . if we generally use
analytical thinking,
we now need
real "Systems Thinking"
to resolve our issues.

—Stephen G. Haines

ebsst1.pmd

1420 Monitor Road • San Diego • California • 92110-1545 • (619) 275-6528 • Fax (619) 275-0324

Why Thinking Matters

The way you think creates the results you get.

The most powerful way to impact the quality of your results is to improve the ways you think.

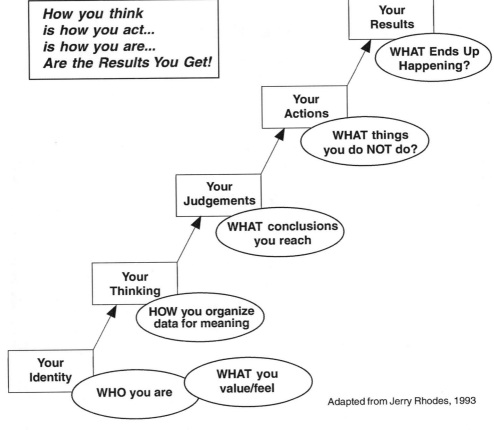

How you think
is how you act...
is how you are...
Are the Results You Get!

Your Results — WHAT Ends Up Happening?

Your Actions — WHAT things you do NOT do?

Your Judgements — WHAT conclusions you reach

Your Thinking — HOW you organize data for meaning

Your Identity — WHO you are — WHAT you value/feel

Adapted from Jerry Rhodes, 1993

ebsst1.pmd

1420 Monitor Road • San Diego • California • 92110-1545 • (619) 275-6528 • Fax (619) 275-0324

A Basic Reorientation of Our Thinking is Needed

In one way or another, we are forced to deal with complexities, with "wholes" or "systems" in all fields of knowledge.

This implies a basic reorientation in "Scientific Thinking"!*

—*Ludwig Van Bertalanffy*

Great Minds

Great Spirits have always encountered violent opposition from mediocre minds...

—*Albert Einstein*

Network of Mutuality

"We are tied together in the single garment of destiny, caught in an inescapable network of mutuality."

—*Martin Luther King*

1420 Monitor Road • San Diego • California • 92110-1545 • (619) 275-6528 • Fax (619) 275-0324

THINKING

We often think about **what** we think

but

we seldom think about **how** we think.

What's the difference?

What are you thinking?

or

How are you thinking?

"As ye thinketh, so shall ye be."
—*Jesus*

"Simply put, change our thoughts, and we can change our world."
—*Prem Chengalath, M.D.*

"The greatest discovery in our lives it that human beings,
by changing the inner attitudes of their minds,
can change the outer aspects of their lives.
—*William James*

Thinking is Hard Work

All the problems of the world could be settled easily if people were only willing to think.

The trouble is that people often resort to all sorts of devices in order not to think, **because thinking is such hard work**.

—Thomas J. Watson

**"If you think you can
...you're right.
If you think you can't
...you're right."**

—*Henry Ford*

The real question is...
"How do you prefer to think?

1420 Monitor Road • San Diego • California • 92110-1545 • (619) 275-6528 • Fax (619) 275-0324

PARADIGMS AND BELIEF SYSTEMS

"Everything that can be invented has been invented."
—Charles H. Duell, Director of U.S. Patent Office, 1899

"Heavier-than-air flying machines are impossible."
—Lord Kelvin, President, Royal Society, 1895

"Sensible and responsible women do not want to vote."
—Grover Cleveland, President, 1905

"Babe Ruth made a mistake when he gave up pitching."
—Tris Speaker, Baseball Player, 1921

"There is no likelihood that man can ever tap the power of the atom."
—Robert Millikan, Nobel Prize winner-Physics, 1923

"Who the hell wants to hear actors talk?"
—Harry Warner, Warner Brothers Pictures, 1927

"I think there is a world market for about five computers."
–Thomas Watson, Chief Executive Office of IBM, 1943

We Impose Limits to Our World View By:

- Language
- Visual
- Frame of Reference
- Psychological
- Cultural
- Personal Bias
- Professional Bias
- What else?

MACHINE–MECHANISTIC VIEW OF THE WORLD (IS OBSOLETE)

DIRECT CAUSE AND EFFECT

I.e.: Acorn ➜ Oak Tree

Cause . . . must be necessary

- Acorn is necessary but not sufficient
- What's missing is the environment ("it all depends)

"Cause and effect" is an environment-free concept

Linear Thinking

Linear thinkers are always looking for a thing or person who is responsible. Systems thinkers take on greater responsibility for events, because their perspective suggests that everyone share responsibility for problems generated by a system.

Source: The Fifth Discipline, Peter M. Senge.

Obsolescence

...as a result of the current paradigm shift, the standard way of doing business is rapidly becoming obsolete and irrelevant.

Unaware

Many remain for me unaware of their own paradigm.

—*Steve Haines*

ebsst1.pmd

1420 Monitor Road • San Diego • California • 92110-1545 • (619) 275-6528 • Fax (619) 275-0324

PARADIGMS — OUR MINDSET — WORLDVIEW

- Paradigms are about patterns of behavior and the rules and regulations we use to construct those patterns.
- We use those patterns:
  - first to establish boundaries, and
  - then to direct us on how to solve problems

Mental Models
We understand the world and take action in it based on notions and assumptions that may reside deeply in the psyche. We may not be aware of the effect these models have on our perception and behavior, yet they have the power to move us forward or hold us back.

Mental models are ways of understanding—or misunderstanding—the world

Source: *The Fifth Discipline,* Peter M. Senge.

Knowing your biases is key to success. Other words used to describe our mindset include:

- worldview
- weltanschauung (German for view of the world)
- paradigms (as popularized by Joel Barker in his videos)
- mental models

> **"Change is Natural"**
>
> "Change is the law of life. And those who look only to the past or present are certain to miss the future."
> —John F. Kennedy

ebsst1.pmd

1420 Monitor Road • San Diego • California • 92110-1545 • (619) 275-6528 • Fax (619) 275-0324

OVERCOMING CONVENTIONAL WISDOM

Overcoming the conventional wisdom was never easy...

For centuries, people believed that Aristotle was right when he said that the heavier an object, the faster it would fall to earth. Aristotle was regarded as the greatest thinker of all times and surely he could not be wrong.

All it would have taken was for one brave person to take two objects, one heavy and one light, and drop them from a great height to see whether or not the heavier object landed first. But no one stepped forward until nearly 2000 years after Aristotle's death.

In 1589, Galileo summoned learned professors to the base of the leaning Tower of Pisa. Then he went to the top and pushed off a ten-pound and a one-pound weight. Both landed at the same time.

But the power of belief in the conventional wisdom was so strong that the professors denied what they had seen. **They continued to say Aristotle was right."**

—Source: *The Executive Speechwriter Newsletter*

EXAMPLES OF PARADIGM SHIFTS

1. Environmental Importance
2. Swiss Watches/Quartz
3. Made in Japan
4. 77 mph Car
5. Solar/Methane Cars/Energy
6. PCs vs. Mainframe Computers
7. Xerox
8. Fax
9. Express Mail
10. Wires vs. Wireless
11. Cellular/Airphone
12. Airplanes vs. Drones
13. Electronics/Internet
14. DVDs and CDs
15. Fall of Berlin Wall
16. Mass Customization/Robotics
17. Global Village
18. Flexible Work Hours/Electronic Cottage Industry
19. Fiber Optics
20. Free Market Socialism vs. Communism
21. 1992 United Europe/Free Trade
22. North America Free Trade/Mercusor
23. Micro Breweries
24. Hong Kong 1997
25. Satellites/Global Communication
26. Business Ethics
27. Participative Management/Empowerment
28. Single Parent vs. Nuclear Family
29. 24-Hour Trading/Work Day
30. Tubes > Transistors > Chips
31. Panama Canal 1999
32. Sickness/Wellness
33. Bio-Technology
34. Bio-Manufacturing

SYSTEMS THINKING—PARADIGM SHIFTS

Obsolescence

...as a result of the current paradigm shift, the standard way of doing business is rapidly becoming obsolete and irrelevant.

Old-Fashioned Industrial Age Concepts	New Systems Age Concepts
Bureaucracy/Functions	Network and Integration
Focus on Institution	Focus on Individuals/Teams
Control	Empowerment
Structure	Flexibility/Minimum Hierarchy
Stability	Change
Self-Sufficiency	Interdependencies
Directive Management	Inspirational Leadership/Vision Shared
Affordable Quality	Value-Added
Personal Security	Personal Growth
Title, Rank, Compensation	Making a Difference
To Compete	To Build and Sustain
Domestic	Global/World Village
Vertical Integration	Alliances/Collaborations
Economy of Scale	Economy of Speed
Single Loop Learning	Double-Loop Learning

If you are doing business now
the same way you did it five years ago,
it's probably obsolete.

—Jack Welch

ebsst1.pmd

1420 Monitor Road • San Diego • California • 92110-1545 • (619) 275-6528 • Fax (619) 275-0324

SYSTEMS — THE NATURAL ORDER OF LIFE ON EARTH

We need to learn:

The Synergy of Systems Solutions

vs.

The Failure of Fragmented Functions

The dominant paradigm in our lives is "Analytic Thinking."

However,

The Natural Order of Life in the World is a *Systems* one.

Thus, analytic approaches (and analytic thinking) to systems problems in everyday life and organizations is now *bankrupt!*

The good news is that this new "Systems Thinking Paradigm" is beginning to emerge; witness the use of new systems-oriented words, such as:

united, fit, integration, collaboration, cooperation, teamwork, partnerships, alliances, linkages, stakeholders, holistic, seamless, boundaryless, system, etc.

Our Systems Model "bridges this gap" — opening up whole new vistas and THE newly emerging paradigm that more properly fits with reality . . . and the **Natural Order of the Universe and Life.**

ebsst1.pmd

1420 Monitor Road • San Diego • California • 92110-1545 • (619) 275-6528 • Fax (619) 275-0324

SYSTEMS AS UNIVERSAL
LAWS OR PRINCIPLES

"You can't cheat Mother Nature"

Simple Analogy—Farmers know natural systems are governed by principles. There is a rhythm and cycle to the seasons of the year and planting and harvesting must follow them to be successful.

Other Universal Laws

- the *life cycle* of "birth, growth, maturity, decline, death" of all living things (people, plants, animals, birds, fish)

- the food chain—on land/in water

- (almost) 24 hours in a day

- balance of nature (i.e., deer/wolves)

- 4 seasons

- 365 (plus) days in a year

- gravity

- male/female roles in procreation

- to survive as human beings we need physical, social, emotional, mental, spiritual stimulation and nourishment

- wind, fire, and sun/moon

- land, water, air

- things get worse before they get better (chaos theory)

If you're not living in harmony with the natural laws and principles of the earth, you won't feel satisfied, be as satisfied or be as successful.

ebsst1.pmd

1420 Monitor Road • San Diego • California • 92110-1545 • (619) 275-6528 • Fax (619) 275-0324

DEFINING STRATEGIC THINKING
(Where is Our Mind Today?)

1. Define Operational Thinking and contrast it to Strategic Thinking.

2. Define Analytical Thinking and contrast it to Strategic Thinking.

3. Define Strategic Planning and contrast it to Strategic Thinking.

4. Define Systems Thinking and contrast it to Strategic Thinking.

ebsst1.pmd

1420 Monitor Road • San Diego • California • 92110-1545 • (619) 275-6528 • Fax (619) 275-0324

STRATEGIC VERSUS
TACTICAL (OPERATIONAL) THINKING/PLANNING

I Thinking/Planning Factors	II Strategic Thinking	III Tactical (Operational) Thinking
1. Time Period?	Longest Period Worth Considering	Shortest Period Worth Considering
2. Reversibility?	Harder	Easier
3. Scope?	Broad	Narrow
4. Affected Areas?	Many Functional Areas	Few Functional Areas
5. Goals?	Means/Ends Also	Means Only

ebsst1.pmd

1420 Monitor Road • San Diego • California • 92110-1545 • (619) 275-6528 • Fax (619) 275-0324

TASK

THE STRATEGY/ OPERATIONS RELATIONSHIP

—Be A Strategic Thinker—

The relationship between strategy and operations can be illustrated in the following way:

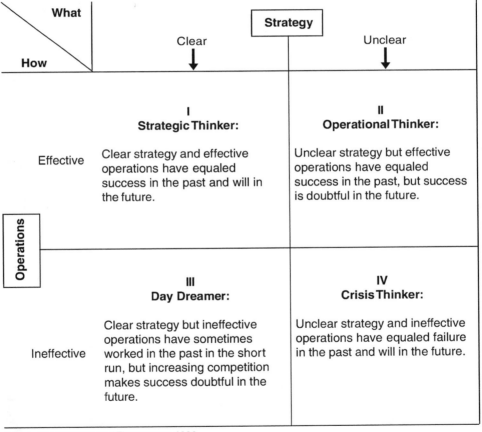

Adapted from Tregoe and Zimmerman, 1980

Question: Which box (I-IV) is your organization in today? Why?

1420 Monitor Road • San Diego • California • 92110-1545 • (619) 275-6528 • Fax (619) 275-0324

THE CRITICAL DIFFERENCE

Strategy   vs.   Tactics

Strategy	Tactics
• central organizing statement	day-to-day actions
• spin put on things	things or tools spun
• road map for marketing plan	vehicles for the trip
• doing the right thing	doing things right
• concept	tools of execution
• organizing glue	what gets glued
• focused	typically, many things
• mental, intangible	physical, sensory
• an "action" statement: verb	things: nouns

"Bridging the Gap"

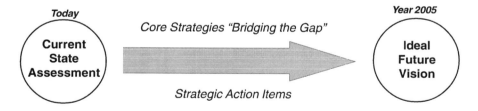

Today

Current State Assessment

Core Strategies "Bridging the Gap"

Strategic Action Items

Year 2005

Ideal Future Vision

Strategy and Priorities

The Purpose of having a strategy is to keep yourself from being seduced by something that is "nice to do."
— Anona Miss

STRATEGIC vs. OPERATIONAL THINKING

Right to Left (Strategic Thinking) = E – A – B

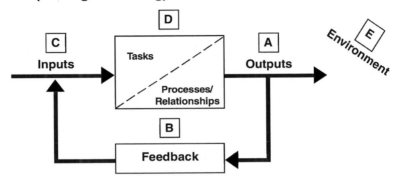

Left to Right (Operational Thinking) = C – D – A

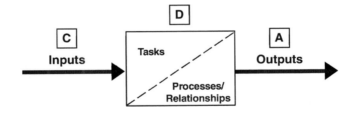

In Sum:

Strategic Thinking is "Backwards Thinking"!

1420 Monitor Road • San Diego • California • 92110-1545 • (619) 275-6528 • Fax (619) 275-0324

SYSTEMS THINKING AND
STRATEGIC THINKING: MEANS → ENDS

Means →

Strategies

Actions

How To/Behaviors

Tasks

Activities

Tactics

Work Plans

Steps

Things We Do

Processes

Major Functions

Throughputs

Ends

Vision

Mission/Purposes

Values/Culture

What

Results

Outputs

Outcomes

Concrete Measures

Goals

Objectives

Key Success Measures

Feedback on Relationships

**Future Environment
Scanning Frequently**

Strategic Thinkers focus on the relationships between means and ends/ measures in their daily work.

1420 Monitor Road • San Diego • California • 92110-1545 • (619) 275-6528 • Fax (619) 275-0324

FOUR LEVELS OF STRATEGIC THINKING

You can be a Strategic Thinker at four levels:

1. Corporate strategy (Enterprise-Wide Positioning)
2. Business unit strategy (competitive strategy)
3. Functional strategy
4. Implementation strategy

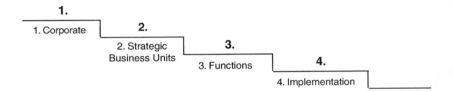

Sole Purpose of Business Enterprises
(To Gain A Competitive Edge)

"What business "Strategy" is all about—what distinguishes it from all other kinds of business planning—in two words, **competitive advantage.**

– Positioning –

Without competitors there would be no need for "Strategy"– for the sole purpose of strategic planning is to design a unique marketplace "Positioning" that will enable your business enterprises to gain a sustainable edge over its competitors."

—*Adapted from Keniche Ohmae*

Strategic Thinkers Focus on their Positioning to Create and Maintain their Competitive Advantage

1420 Monitor Road • San Diego • California • 92110-1545 • (619) 275-6528 • Fax (619) 275-0324

WORLD-CLASS STAR POSITIONING

YOUR COMPETITIVE BUSINESS EDGE – CREATING CUSTOMER VALUE

C = Personal Choice
Fashion, Control, Self, Customized, Tailored, Variety, Individuality, My/Me, Comprehensive Choices, Mass Customization

S = Caring Service
Personal Service, Values, Feeling Important, Customer Relationships, Respect, Caring, Emotions, Recovery Strategy, Integrity, Empathy, Sensitivity, Familiar, Trust, Cultural

Q = High Quality (Products & Services)
Features, Authentic, Simplicity, Information, Technology, Accuracy, Knowledge, Performance, Reliability, Functional, Durability, Uses, Consistency, Stability, Soundness, Unique, Experiences, Innovative

R = Responsiveness
Fast Delivery, Convenience, Methods, Timing, Distribution, Flexibility, Access, Ease of Doing Business, Support Services, Cooperation

T = Total Cost
Psychological Cost, Price, Life Cycle, Risk, Opportunity Costs, Waste/Environment, Working Conditions, Product/Services Costs

Service

Customer

CREATING CUSTOMER VALUE

$$\text{Brand/Recognition/Positioning} = \text{Perceived Customer Value} = \frac{\text{Outputs}}{\text{Inputs}} = \frac{\text{What I Get}}{\text{What I Must Give}} = \textbf{Benefits}$$

Star.eps

ebsst1.pmd

1420 Monitor Road • San Diego • California • 92110-1545 • (619) 275-6528 • Fax (619) 275-0324

THE COMPETITIVE POSITIONING STATEMENT

Also called: Positioning – Driving Force – Grand Strategy – Competitive Edge/Advantage – Strategic Intent – Image – Reputation – Identity – Value Proposition

- Defines our Driving Force(s) as **"the way we differentiate ourselves"** vs. the competition. Sometimes called "the mother of all Core Strategies" as it defines "how we are driven" as an organization.

- It is the main way we achieve a sustained competitive advantage/edge vs. the competition over time.

- Our Rallying Cry is derived from, and reinforces, this position.

- Requires that we be a "monomaniac with a mission" over time to make this our distinctive competency and reputation.

- *Note:* customer-focused/oriented organizations do this via 1 of the 5 points on the World-Class Star (★) Positioning model of customer wants/needs.

- Be sure you are **not** noncompetitive (i.e., are "ballpark competitive") in all other key areas of customer wants and needs.

- If a Competitive Positioning Statement is already incorporated in your organization's Mission Statement, you may not need to complete this page. However, having a clearly defined Positioning Statement, that stands on its own, is critically important in setting a clear direction for your organization's future.

ebsst1.pmd

1420 Monitor Road • San Diego • California • 92110-1545 • (619) 275-6528 • Fax (619) 275-0324

SYSTEMS THINKING = STRATEGIC THINKING

is also:
- Critical Thinking
- Solutions Thinking
- Future and Forward Thinking
- Longer-Term Thinking
- High-Level Thinking

…Rather than analytic thinking, which is tactical, mechanistic, reductionistic, and either/or thinking (parts oriented; one best way)

Why?

Because Systems Thinking focuses on:

- Relationships
- Multiple Outcomes
- Holism and Boundaries
- The Environment
- The Larger System
- Feedback

Strategic Thinking:

It's about:

- Clarity and Simplicity • Meaning and Purpose
- Focus and Direction

Desired Outcomes • Relationships and Feedback!

ebsst1.pmd

1420 Monitor Road • San Diego • California • 92110-1545 • (619) 275-6528 • Fax (619) 275-0324

STRATEGIC THINKING DEFINED

Strategic Thinking **is a broader and more innovative way of thinking** on a daily basis about the overall goals of your job, team, and organization. It is longer-term oriented with a more system and holistic view of your environment.

It is also **disciplined thinking** with a focus first on the desired outcomes of your entire business as a system, and then on the relationships between your organizational components along with constant feedback on results to find the leverage points that best achieve your **desired outcomes.**

STRATEGIC "PLANNING" DEFINED

Strategic Planning **is a dynamic "backwards thinking" process** by the collective leadership of an organization . . .

- to define their *ideal future vision* (i.e., "ends planning") and the core directional statements required . . .

- for consistent and meaningful annual operating plans and budgets . . .

- that drive the measurement and achievement of the future vision.

The strategic plan itself is a blueprint. The annual plans and budgets have the specific yearly details.

Question: **What are the key words/phrases in this definition? Why**

STRATEGIC THINKING FURTHER DEFINED

The parts of an organization don't usually fit and work together well:

- Strategic Thinking is about clarifying the Direction and Vision of the whole – and its success measures.

- Strategic Thinking is about identifying relationships supporting the whole.

- Strategic Thinking is about identifying leverage points for change.

----

1. This is a **simple yet structured way to organize your thoughts** about all the complexity in your world today.

2. So that you **clarify your goals, desired outcomes or vision** you want the whole system to achieve...along with constant feedback vs. the desired outcomes.

3. So that the **relationships and fit of the parts** and pieces to each other are supporting , not hindering, achievement of the whole.

4. So that you can **clarify where the leverage is** for successful change.

5. Leading to a **powerful synergy of people working together** to achieve the same common goals of vision in a **better and superior way**.

**"THIS" IS SYSTEMS THINKING
IT IS ALSO STRATEGIC THINKING**

1420 Monitor Road • San Diego • California • 92110-1545 • (619) 275-6528 • Fax (619) 275-0324

STRATEGIC AND SYSTEMS THINKING

SUMMARY:

I. Scientific Foundation: The way to think is Systems Thinking

II. Applications:

1. Reinventing Strategic Planning – overall direction
2. Strategic Thinking – daily, based on overall direction
3. Strategic Management – yearly cycle
   (Strategic Planning + Strategic Thinking + Leadership + Change + Innovation)

III. Outcomes:

= Business Excellence

= Superior Results

TASK

ANALYTICAL THINKING (AND SPECIALIZATION)

("Micro Right—Macro Wrong")

1. IRS Rules—over 4000 pages

2. Health Care—thousands of small specialized entities based on singular type grants

3. Social Services—thousands of small specialized entities based on singular categorical type grants

4. Specialized Government Districts—water districts, assessment districts, school districts, etc.

5. Separate Cities and Counties—little or no geographic separation

6. Federal Intelligence Agencies—16 of them

7. Congressional Subcommittees—too numerous to mention

8. California—7,700 page education code

9. U.S. Naval Academy regulations (from 10 to 1000+ pages in 150 years)

10. Sears—29,000 pages of policies and procedures

11. Federal Government Policies and Procedures—Al Gore's "Stacks and Stacks."

What else can you think of?

12.

13.

14.

Does this kind of control really work? What are the alternatives?

1420 Monitor Road • San Diego • California • 92110-1545 • (619) 275-6528 • Fax (619) 275-0324

SYSTEMS AND ANALYTIC THINKING

Fact

The kind of thinking and strategies/actions we generally use today in our social systems has led to both:

1. spectacular successes, and
2. spectacular failures (huge/intractable chronic problems we can't seem to solve).

Why?

Hypothesis

1. The way we think has something to do with it.
2. Adding an understanding and use of systems thinking will improve the probability of better problem solving and solution seeking.

We need to use systems thinking and analytic thinking and systems thinking again (in that order)

Systems Thinking Approach

1. First look at the whole system and its interactions in its environment.
2. Second, analyze the parts of the system for their performance and then synthesize their impact back on and support for maximizing the whole.

Thus, the key is optimizing the parts to maximize the whole system.

Analytic and systems thinking are both important.

Their similarities include:

- They are both ways of thinking in a disciplined fashion.
- They help each other look at both the parts and the whole.
- They are both helpful and practical ways to deal with problems and issues.
- What else?

ebsst1.pmd

SYSTEMS VS. ANALYTIC THINKING

—THREE STEPS—

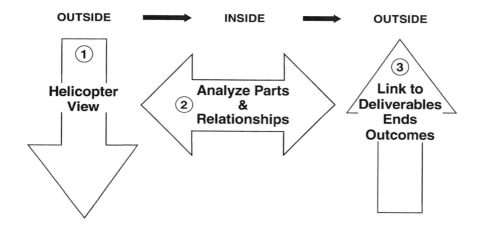

| OUTSIDE | → | INSIDE | → | OUTSIDE |

① Helicopter View

② Analyze Parts & Relationships

③ Link to Deliverables Ends Outcomes

1420 Monitor Road • San Diego • California • 92110-1545 • (619) 275-6528 • Fax (619) 275-0324

CHANGING OUR THINKING?

Systems Defined
Systems are made up of a set of components that work together for the overall objective of the whole (output).

Systems Thinking . . .
is finding patterns and relationships, and learning to reinforce or change these patterns to fulfill your vision and mission.

Systemic Change . . .
is change that relates to or affects the entire body or system.

In Short . . .
the world can no longer be comprehended as a simple machine. It is a complex, highly interconnected system.

The Basic Trouble . . .
is that most people are still trying to solve the problems of a complex system with the mentality and tools that were appropriate for the world as a . . .

Simple Machine

—Ian Mitroff

ebsst1.pmd

1420 Monitor Road • San Diego • California • 92110-1545 • (619) 275-6528 • Fax (619) 275-0324

SYSTEMS THINKING—A BETTER LANGUAGE

(AND A BETTER WAY OF BEING)

Systems thinking principles are like a wide-angle lens on a camera. They give you a better view on your "radar scope" and thus **a more effective way of thinking, communicating, problem solving, acting, and achieving superior results!**

— Otherwise —

> "Today's thinking (and problem solving)
>
> is the source
>
> of tomorrow's problems."

Discovery

"Discovery consists in seeing
what everyone else has seen
and thinking what no one
else has thought."

—*Albert Szent-Gyorgi*

**"The Quality of an organization can
never exceed the Quality of the minds
that make it up."**

—*Harold R. McAlindon*

1420 Monitor Road • San Diego • California • 92110-1545 • (619) 275-6528 • Fax (619) 275-0324

SHIFTING VIEW OF THE WORLD
THROUGH CHANGING THOUGHT PATTERNS

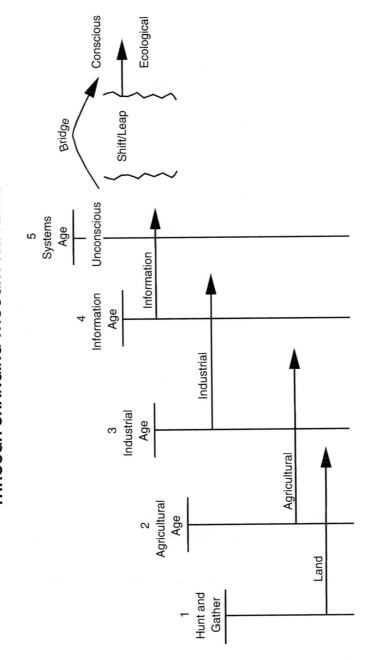

1420 Monitor Road • San Diego • California • 92110-1545 • (619) 275-6528 • Fax (619) 275-0324

PARADIGM SHIFT TO SYSTEMS THINKING

Mental Models

Worldview

Basic Assumptions

or

Weltanschauung (German)

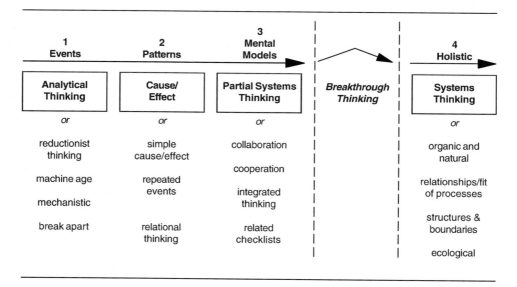

1 Events	2 Patterns	3 Mental Models		4 Holistic
Analytical Thinking	**Cause/ Effect**	**Partial Systems Thinking**	*Breakthrough Thinking*	**Systems Thinking**
or	*or*	*or*		*or*
reductionist thinking	simple cause/effect	collaboration		organic and natural
machine age	repeated events	cooperation		relationships/fit of processes
mechanistic		integrated thinking		
break apart	relational thinking	related checklists		structures & boundaries
				ecological

This is a shift from seeing elements, functions and events

to ...

seeing the processes, structures, and interrelationship of them to each other

and their desired outcomes.

1420 Monitor Road • San Diego • California • 92110-1545 • (619) 275-6528 • Fax (619) 275-0324

GENERAL SYSTEMS THEORY – SCIENCE-BASED

The Only Science-Based Research in the Management Field!

...is not a theory but the **natural laws** of life on earth just like:

- mathematical laws
- laws of physics
- laws of thermodynamics

BFO
(**B**linding **F**lash of the **O**bvious)

It's the system, stupid!

but

We are blind to the system—it's too obvious

"Nothing is so practical as a good theory."

—*Jerry Harvey (thanks to Kurt Lewin)*

"A 'scientific basis is even better."

—*Stephen Haines*

Systems Theory Examples

- Three blind men and an elephant
- World's best car example
- Doctor's traditional injury treatment
- Medicine and pills—their by-products
- Ripple effect of a stone thrown into water
- Physical stress vs. emotions vs. illness
- Employee treatment vs. customer service
- "9-11" vs. Travel Industry Collapses

"Behavioral Science" has a scientific basis too – about people!

GENERAL SYSTEMS THEORY – SCIENCE-BASED

I am wary of the word "system" because . . . "system" is a highly cathectic term, loaded with prestige.

Hence, we are all strongly tempted to employ it even when we have nothing definite in mind and its only service is to indicate that we subscribe to the general premise respecting the interdependence of things.

—Kast and Rosenzweig
quoting the psychologist, Murray

The Failure of the Quick Fix
Doing the most obvious quick fix
usually
does not produce the most obvious desired outcome.

The words "General Systems Theory" imply that some things can usefully be said about systems in general, despite the immense diversity of their specific forms.

One of these things should be a scheme of classification.

Every science begins by classifying its subject matter, if only descriptively, and learns a lot about it in the process; and systems especially need this attention, because an adequate classification cuts across familiar boundaries and at the same time draws valid and important distinctions which have previously been sensed but not defined.

In short, the task of GST is to find the most general conceptual framework in which a scientific theory or a technological problem can be placed without losing the essential features of the theory or the problem.

—Geoffrey Vickers, 1970

ebsst1.pmd

1420 Monitor Road • San Diego • California • 92110-1545 • (619) 275-6528 • Fax (619) 275-0324

GENERAL SYSTEMS THEORY (GST)

- ## The Laws of Biological Systems

Since the fundamental character of the living thing is its organization, the customary investigation of the single parts and processes cannot provide a complete explanation of the vital phenomena. This investigation gives us no information about the coordination of parts and processes.

Thus the chief task of biology must be to discover **the laws of biological systems** (at all levels of organization). We believe that the attempts to find a foundation for theoretical biology point at a fundamental change in the world picture. This view, considered as a method of investigation, we shall call "organismic biology" and, as an attempt at an explanation, "the system of the organism."

—Ludwig von Bertalanffy

Quoted in 1972 in "General Systems Theory Yearbook"

- ## General Principles of Systems

There exists models, principles, and laws that apply to generalized systems or their subclasses irrespective of their particular kind, the nature of the component elements, and the relations or "forces" between them. We postulate a new discipline called *General Systems Theory*.

General Systems Theory is a logico-mathematical field whose task is the formulation and derivation of those **general principles that are applicable to "systems" in general**. In this way, exact formulations of terms such as wholeness and sum, differentiation, progressive mechanization, centralization, hierarchal order, finality and equifinality, etc., becomes possible, terms which occur in all sciences dealing with "systems" and imply their logical homology.

—George J. Klir

THE SYSTEMS THINKING APPROACH^{SM}

"The Only Macro-Scientific, Heavily Researched, and Natural (Holistic) Way to Think"

Based on:

1. Biological research on Living Systems, started in the 1920s by Ludwig Von Bertalanffy (1901-1972). He was the intellectual Titan of the 20th Century – now better understood in the 21st Century.

    His disciplines were biology, medicine, psychiatry, psychology, sociology, history, education and philosophy.

    His lifetime goal: A Unity of Science – for all living systems on earth.

2. The resulting "Society for General Systems Research" (SGSR) formed in the fall of 1954, Palo Alto, California by four prestigious interdisciplinary thinkers:
    *   Ludwig von Bertalanffy—Biology
    *   Anatol Rapoport—Applied Math/Philosopher
    *   Ralph Gerard—Physiologist
    *   Kenneth Boulding—Economist
    *   Note: Some say there were others, such as the anthropologist Margaret Mead.

3. As articulated in the annual yearbooks of this Society (1956—1970s), as well as the teachings and writings of renaissance professors of management, such as:
    *   Russ Ackoff—University of Pennsylvania
    *   Jay Forrester/Peter Senge—Massachusetts Institute of Technology (MIT)
    *   Gene Ericson—George Washington University
    *   and many more

4. By the 1980s, there were over 1000 members of the SGSR—in 11 Universities and 23 countries

5. And as interpreted and translated **for the first time** into practical management tools by Stephen G. Haines, President and Founder of the Centre for Strategic Management®.

Other associated concepts and theories imbedded as part of General Systems Theory include:

1. Socio-Technical Systems Theory (England 1960s)
2. Complexity Theory (Various in the 1990's)
3. Chaos Theory (Fritjof Capra and others)
4. Quantum Theory (Mark Youngblood)
5. Self-Organizing Systems (Margaret Wheatley)
6. Mental Models (Peter Senge)
7. What else?

Our Systems Thinking Goal:
"Find and apply the Unity of Science and its Natural Laws to improve life
as it relates to Living Systems here on Earth"

---

ebsst1.pmd

1420 Monitor Road • San Diego • California • 92110-1545 • (619) 275-6528 • Fax (619) 275-0324

The Broad Systems Thinking Field

Interrelationships of Processes

It includes cybernetics, chaos theory, gestalt theory, general systems theory, complexity theory, socio-technical systems, systems change, as well as computers, telecommunications, project management and the work of Gregory Bateson, Russell Ackoff, Eric Trist, Ludwig von Bertalanffy.

All of these diverse approaches have one guiding idea in common: **behavior of all living systems follows certain common and natural principles, the nature of which are being discovered and articulated.**

From Events to Interrelationships

A pragmatic view of systems thinking is that it is a body of tools and methodology for solving difficult, highly interdependent problems. But ultimately, it is about expanding our worldview.

This shift in orientation—from objects and events to interrelationships—must infiltrate broadly and deeply if it is to start to have a real cultural impact.

— The Systems Thinker,
August 1994

See the World Anew

Systems thinking is a discipline for seeing wholes, a framework for seeing patterns and interrelationships.

It's especially important to see the world as a whole as it grows more and more complex. Complexity can overwhelm and undermine: "It's the system. I have no control."

Systems thinking makes these realities more manageable; **it's the antidote for feelings of helplessness.**

By seeing the patterns that lie behind events and details, we can actually simplify life.

—Peter M. Senge
The Fifth Discipline

ebsst1.pmd

1420 Monitor Road • San Diego • California • 92110-1545 • (619) 275-6528 • Fax (619) 275-0324

THE POWER OF PROFOUND KNOWLEDGE
(W. Edwards Deming)

To provide you with a better understanding of Profound Knowledge as Dr. W. Edwards Deming had proposed, it consists of four elements:

1. **Theory of Systems.** Systems and Processes are synonymous. I present and compare the various views of systems theory from Zadeh, Von Bertanlaffy, Kauffman, Ackoff, Senge and Powers. I use "I Think" simulations to show the dynamics of positive and negative feedback loops

2. **Theory of Variation.** Variation is everywhere. I present the various views of variation from Deming, Wheeler, and Scherkenbach. I use animation and simulations to show the importance of prediction given knowledge of variation

3. **Theory of Knowledge (Learning).** "This should have been the most important course that you ever attended." I present the various views of epistemology from Pierce, Lewis, James Bridgman, Kuhn and Gilovich. I build on the theories of systems and variation to expand on previous epistemologies

4. **Theory of Psychology.** Everybody wants to feel important. I present the various views of psychology from Frankl, Ryan and Oestreich, McGregor, Watzlawick, Weakland and Fisch, and Tannen. I discuss actions that you might take on physical, logical and emotional levels to help people feel important as an individual or as a part of a team

There is a detailed framework from various bodies of knowledge that shows the interdependence of all four elements.

The "Law of Linkage" States:

—Bill Jensen

Integrating the various parts of our work efforts—employee empowerment, risk-taking, innovation, process improvement, quality, and leadership's "walking the talk"—will have a far greater effect on employee behavior than perfecting any one or two of these efforts alone.

Source: *Strategy & Leadership*, March/April 1997

---

ebsst1.pmd

1420 Monitor Road • San Diego • California • 92110-1545 • (619) 275-6528 • Fax (619) 275-0324

SYSTEMS:

Doing Better Today Than You Did Yesterday

— W. Edwards Deming (1982)

—*Inc.*, December 1996

Deming's entire approach stands in stark contrast to faddishness, and I'm distressed by the number of companies that have adopted techniques and tools of the quality movement without embracing the philosophy of continuous improvement.

For Deming, continuous improvement was not a bag of tricks but a way of life—a zen-like discipline to be practiced day in and day out. It requires an unwavering commitment to facing everyday with the question, What **can we do better today than we did yesterday?** There is no finish line, no "we've arrived." In Deming's world, you never arrive. You can always do better, and you should never stop the process of improvement.

Deming's perspective reflects a more Eastern habit of mind. In the Western world, we seek to affix blame and reward to individuals. **Deming teaches that we** must **reject that lens and look instead at the** *system* **in which individuals operate.**

To improve quality, fix the system, where 95% of the problems lie.

THE SCANS REPORT:

—Margaret Riel

PREPARING STUDENTS FOR THEIR FUTURE

Working backwards from the end point is one of the problem-solving strategies that students learn in school. In the 1990s, the Department of Labor applied this strategy to the problem of redesigning our schools. They turned to industry and business and asked them: **"What does work require of schools?"**

Lynne Martin, former Secretary of Labor, formed the **Secretary's Commission on Achieving Necessary Skills (SCANS)** to find the answer to this question.

The SCANS commission identified three foundational skills and five competencies.

The Three SCANS Foundational Skills

#1   *Basic Skill Development:* Reading, writing, arithmetic, mathematics, speaking and listening.

* #2   ***Thinking Skills:*** Thinking creatively making decisions, solving problems, visualizing, learning how to learn and reason.

#3   *Personal Qualities:* Individual responsibility, self-esteem, sociability, self-management, and integrity.

The Five SCANS Competencies

#1   *Resources:* Allocating time, money, materials, space, and staff.

#2   *Interpersonal Skills:* Working on teams, teaching others, serving customers, leading, negotiating, and working well with people from culturally diverse backgrounds.

#3   *Information Handling Skills:* Acquiring and evaluating data, organizing and maintaining files, interpreting and communicating, and computer processing of information.

* #4   ***Systems:*** Understanding social, organizational and technological systems, monitoring performance, and designing and improving systems.

#5   *Technology:* Selecting appropriate technology, applying the most effective tools for the task, and using good troubleshooting skills.

Source: *T.I.E. News,* Volume 5, Number 1

ebsst1.pmd

1420 Monitor Road • San Diego • California • 92110-1545 • (619) 275-6528 • Fax (619) 275-0324

ALL SCIENTIFIC DISCIPLINES

SCIENCES "CONVERGING ON" SYSTEMS THINKING

Past/Current fields/disciplines trending towards Systems Thinking

1. Cybernetics (Norbert Wiener)
2. Chaos Theory (Jack Cohen, Glenda Eoyang, James Gleick)
3. Gestalt Therapy (Fritz Perls)
4. General Systems Theory (Von Bertalanffy)
5. Complexity Theory (Stuart Kauffman)
6. Socio--Technical Systems Theory (Eric Trist)
7. Project Managers (Various)
8. Information Systems (Various)
9. TQM (Deming, Juran)
10. Operations Research, (Military)
11. Geodesic Domes (Buckminster Fuller)
12. Physics (Fritjof Capra, Murray Gell-Mann)
13. Mind and Nature (Gregory Bateson)
14. Systems Thinking (Russell Ackoff)
15. The Structure of Scientific Revolution (Thomas Kuhn)
16. Organization Development (Barry Oshry, Kathleen Dannemiller)
17. Human Resource Management (Robert Brinkerhoff)
18. Biology (David Wann, von Bertalanffy)
19. Systems Dynamics (Jay Forrester)
20. Mathematics (Jay Forrester)
21. Self-Organized Systems (Margaret Wheatley)
22. Astronomers
23. Neuroscientists
24. Philosophers (Russell Ackoff)
25. Economists (Roger Terry, Michael Rothschild)
26. Futurists (Joel Barker, John Naisbitt)
27. Educators Richard Herrnstein, Jeanette Vos)
28. Modern Artists (Tyler Volk)
29. Architects (Many)
30. Mythology (James Moore)
31. Leadership (Meg Wheatley/ Centre for Strategic Management)
32. Business/Management (Peter Drucker)
33. Atmospheric and Oceanographic Sciences
34. Strategic Planning (Steve Haines)
35. Government (Alice Rivlin)35) Psychology (Steven Covey)
36. Community Development (Don Eberly)
37. Spiritual (Various)
38. Chiropractors (Gary Bretow)
39. The Learning Organization (Peter Senge)
40. Health Care (Plexus Institute)
41. Physiology (Ralph Gerard
42. Quantum Theory (Mark Youngblood)
43. Soft Systems Methodology (Peter Checkland)
44. Accelerated Learning (Dr. Georgi Lozanov)

ebsst1.pmd

1420 Monitor Road • San Diego • California • 92110-1545 • (619) 275-6528 • Fax (619) 275-0324

THE SYSTEMS THINKING APPROACH^SM

RAISE YOUR STRATEGIC I.Q. 50 POINTS

—Compliments of Ludwig Von Bertalanffy

- A new "Orientation to Life"; simplicity
- A different, better way to think
- A higher order of thinking
- An advanced way of thinking and advanced form of intelligence
- A higher intellect —more integrative of parts/more relational
- More systematic and strategic in your thinking; better diagnostic tools
- Is key to critical thinking and strategic thinking
- A macro-scientific and transdisciplinary framework; common language
- Is towards a "Unity of Science"
- Is how to: out-think...out-flank...and out-maneuver the competition
- Is the top two stages of maturity below:

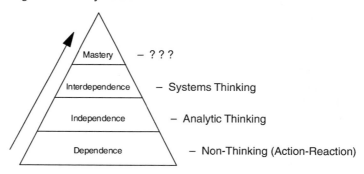

Mastery	– ? ? ?
Interdependence	– Systems Thinking
Independence	– Analytic Thinking
Dependence	– Non-Thinking (Action-Reaction)

In Summary:
- We are governed by the natural laws of life and living as open/living systems on earth.

—so—

- **A successful participant must learn the rules**

- **Analytical thinking is old Industrial Revolution thinking.**

1420 Monitor Road • San Diego • California • 92110-1545 • (619) 275-6528 • Fax (619) 275-0324

IN SUMMARY

Our Belief

The Systems Thinking Approach[SM] is an absolute necessity to make sense of and succeed in today's complex world.

If life on earth is governed by the natural laws of living systems, then a successful participant should learn the rules.

—*Stephen G. Haines*
1998

Become A Strategic & Systems Thinker!

1420 Monitor Road • San Diego • California • 92110-1545 • (619) 275-6528 • Fax (619) 275-0324

KEY CONCEPTS OF GENERAL
SYSTEMS THEORY — "NATURAL LAWS"

(AND THEIR "SYSTEM DYNAMICS" IN ORGANIZATIONS)

I. THE WHOLE SYSTEM

1. **Holism, Synergism Organicism, and Gestalt**
   The whole is not just the sum of the parts; **the system itself can be explained only as a totality.**

   Holism is the opposite of elementarism, which views the total as the sum of its individual parts.

2. **Open Systems View**
   Systems can be considered in two ways: (1) closed, or (2) open. Open systems exchange information, energy, or material with their environment.

   Biological and social systems are inherently open systems; mechanical systems may be open or closed. The concepts of open and closed systems are difficult to defend in the absolute.

   We prefer to think of open-closed as a dimension; that is, **systems are relatively open or relatively closed.**

3. **Systems Boundaries**
   It follows that systems have boundaries which separate them from their environments. The concept of boundaries helps us understand the distinction between open and closed systems. The relatively closed system has rigid, impenetrable boundaries; whereas the open system has permeable boundaries between itself and a broader suprasystem.

   Boundaries are relatively easily defined in physical and biological systems, but are **very difficult to delineate in social systems, such as organizations.**

4. **Input–Transformation–Output Model**
   The open system can be viewed as a transformation model.

   In a dynamic relationship with its environment, it receives various inputs, transforms these inputs in some way, and exports outputs.

5. **Feedback**
   The concept of feedback is important in understanding how a system maintains a steady state.

   Information concerning the outputs or the process of the system is fed back as an input into the system, perhaps leading to changes in the transformation process and/or future outputs.

   Feedback can be both positive and negative, although the field of cybernetics is based on negative feedback. Negative feedback is information input which indicates that the system is deviating from a prescribed course and should readjust to a new steady state.

6. **Multiple Goal-Seeking**
   Biological and social systems appear to have multiple goals or purposes.

   Social organizations seek multiple goals, if for no other reason than that they are composed of individuals and subunits with different values and objectives.

continued

1420 Monitor Road • San Diego • California • 92110-1545 • (619) 275-6528 • Fax (619) 275-0324

KEY CONCEPTS OF GENERAL
SYSTEMS THEORY — "NATURAL LAWS"

II. THE INNER WORKINGS

7. Equifinality of Open Systems
In mechanistic systems there is a direct cause and effect relationship between the initial conditions and the final state. **Biological and social systems operate differently.**

Equifinality suggests that certain results may be achieved with different initial conditions and in different ways.

This view suggests that social organizations can accomplish their objectives with diverse inputs and with varying internal activities (conversation processes).

8. Entropy
Closed, physical systems are subject to the force of entropy which increases until eventually the entire system fails.

The tendency toward maximum entropy is a movement to disorder, complete lack of resource transformation, and death.

In a closed system, the change in entropy must always be positive; however, in open biological or social systems, entropy can be arrested and may even be transformed into negative entropy— a process of more complete organization and ability to transform resources—**because the system imports resources from its environment.**

9. Hierarchy
A basic concept in systems thinking is that of hierarchical relationships between systems.

A system is composed of subsystems of a lower order and is also part of a suprasystem.

Thus, there is a hierarchy of the components of the system.

10. Subsystems or Components
A system by definition is composed of interrelated parts or elements. This is true for all systems— mechanical, biological, and social.

Every system has at least two elements and these elements are interconnected.

11. Steady State, Dynamic Equilibrium
The concept of steady state is closely related to that of negative entropy. A closed system eventually must attain an equilibrium state with maximum entropy—death or disorganization.

However, an open system may attain a state where the system remains in dynamic equilibrium through the continuous inflow of materials, energy, and information.

12. Internal Elaboration
Closed systems move toward entropy and disorganization.

In contrast, open systems appear to move in the direction of greater differentiation, elaboration, and a higher level of organization.

Source: adapted from *Academy of Management Journal*, December 1972 by Stephen G. Haines

SYSTEMS THINKING'S NATURAL LAWS

(Life Here on Earth for All Living Systems)

12 Natural Laws   -and-   Their Best Practices

I. The Whole System

1. Holism	1. Ask "What's your purpose"? (No. 1 Systems Question)
2. Open System	2. Scan the environment regularly (Ask implications)
3. Boundaries	3. Collaborate across them (Seek win—win)
4. Input/Output	4. Use "Backwards Thinking" (Learn your A-B-Cs)
5. Feedback (is a gift)	5. Encourage "gifts"
6. Multiple Outcomes	6. Organizational and individual outcomes (WIIFM)—(acknowledge both)

II. The Inner Workings

7. Equifinality	7. Empower the means (Focus on ends, not means)
8. Entropy	8. Build in Booster Shots
9. Hierarchy	9. Flatten the Hierarchy
10. Relationships	10. Recognize Relationships and Fit
11. Dynamic Equilibrium	11. Blast away the ruts
12. Internal Elaboration	12. Create Clarity and Simplicity

ebsst2.pmd

1420 Monitor Road • San Diego • California • 92110-1545 • (619) 275-6528 • Fax (619) 275-0324

THE SIMPLICITY OF SYSTEMS THINKING℠

FIVE KEY PHASES: The A-B-C-D-E Systems Model

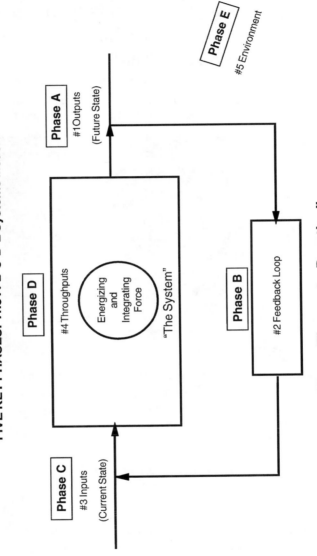

Phase A
#1 Outputs
(Future State)

Phase E
#5 Environment

Phase D
#4 Throughputs
Energizing and Integrating Force
"The System"

Phase B
#2 Feedback Loop

Phase C
#3 Inputs
(Current State)

"From Theory to Practice"

Systems: Systems are made up of a set of components that work together for the overall objective of the whole (output).

"A New Orientation to Life"—Our Core Technology

ebsst2.pmd

1420 Monitor Road • San Diego • California • 92110-1545 • (619) 275-6528 • Fax (619) 275-0324

THE SYSTEMS THINKING APPROACH℠

"A New Orientation to Life" – Our Core Technology
STRATEGIC THINKING
"From Complexity to Simplicity"

Systems: Systems are made up of a set of components that work together for the overall objective of the whole (output).

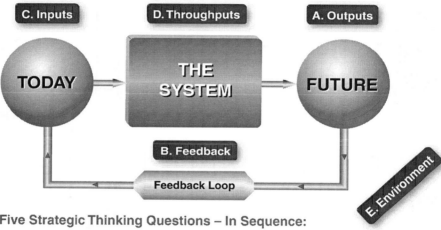

Five Strategic Thinking Questions – In Sequence:

A Where do we want to be? (i.e., our ends, outcomes, purposes, goals, holistic vision)

B How will we know when we get there? (i.e., the customers' needs and wants connected into a quantifiable feedback system)

C Where are we now? (i.e., today's issues and problems)

D How do we get there? (i.e., close the gap from C → A in a complete, holistic way)

E Ongoing:
What will/may change in your environment in the future?

vs. Analytic Thinking *Which:*

① Starts with today and the current state, issues, and problems.

② Breaks the issues and/or problems into their smallest components.

③ Solves each component separately (i.e., maximizes the solution).

④ Has no far-reaching vision or goal (just the absence of the problem).

NOTE: In Systems Thinking, the Whole is Primary and the Parts are Secondary (not vice-versa).

"If you don't know where you're going, any road will get you there."

ebsst2.pmd

1420 Monitor Road • San Diego • California • 92110-1545 • (619) 275-6528 • Fax (619) 275-0324

SYSTEMS — THE INNER WORKINGS

FROM THE 12 NATURAL LAWS OF LIVING SYSTEMS

E Future Environment

A OUTPUTS

D Open System Boundaries

WEB OF RELATIONSHIPS

Entropy

Hierarchy — EQUILIBRIUM — Internal Elaboration

DYNAMIC

Equifinality

B Feedback Loop

C INPUTS

ebsst2.pmd

innerworkings.eps

1420 Monitor Road • San Diego • California • 92110-1545 • (619) 275-6528 • Fax (619) 275-0324

PROPERTIES OF SYSTEMS – BE STRATEGIC

Systems Thinking…is finding patterns and relationships, and learning to reinforce or change these patterns to fulfill your vision and mission.

1. **The Whole is Primary**—The whole is primary and the parts are secondary. Focusing on maximizing the parts leads to suboptimizing the whole

2. **Understand Systems Holistically in Their Environment**—Systems, and organizations as systems, can only be understood holistically. Try to understand the system and its environment first. Organizations are open systems and, as such, are viable only in mutual interaction with and adaptation to the changing environment

3. **Each System Functions Uniquely**—Every system has properties/functions that none of its parts can do

4. **System Purposes First**—The place to start is with the whole and its purposes within its environment. The parts and their relationships evolve from this

5. **The Role of Parts—Supports the Whole**—Parts play their role in light of the purpose for which the whole exists. Focus on the desired outcomes; not just the problems of the parts

6. **All Parts Are Interdependent**—Parts, elements, subsystems are interdependent…a web of relationships. Therefore, yesterday's great solutions may lead to today's issues. Every system cannot be subdivided into independent parts; a system as a whole cannot function effectively when it loses a part

7. **Small Changes Produce Big Results**—Change in any element of a system effects the whole as well as the other elements, subsystems. The small changes can produce big results if the leverage points are clear

8. **Maximizing Parts Suboptimizes the Whole**—Exclusive focus on one element or subsystem without simultaneous attention to other subsystems leads to suboptimal results and new disturbances. The solution or simple cure can often be worse than the real disease

9. **Causes and Effects Are Not Closely Related**—Delay time and delayed reactions along with cause and effect being not closely related in time and space cause inaccurate diagnoses and solutions. Direct cause and effect is an environmentally free concept

ebsst2.pmd

1420 Monitor Road • San Diego • California • 92110-1545 • (619) 275-6528 • Fax (619) 275-0324

PROPERTIES OF SYSTEMS

10. **Faster is Ultimately Slower**—Systems have a natural pace to them. Sometimes trying to go faster is ultimately slower

11. **Feedback and Boundaries**—Systems are more "open" and likely to sustain their existence longer and more effectively, the more feedback they receive from the environment through all aspects of their boundaries

12. **Multiple Goals**—All social systems have multiple goals; building consensus on them first is the key to successful teamwork and achieving these goals

13. **Equifinality and Flexibility**—People can achieve their goals and outcomes in many different styles/ways—thus the CSM "strategic consistency – operational flexibility" concept of the '90s

14. **Hierarchy is Natural**—Despite some recent political correctness against hierarchies, all systems have a natural hierarchy; find it, minimize it, and make it work for you

15. **Entropy and Tendency to Run Down**—All systems have a tendency towards maximum entropy, disorder and death. Importing resources from the environment is key to long-term viability, closed systems move toward this disorganization faster than open systems

So: A system cannot be understood by analysis—but by synthesis—looking at it as a whole within its environment

Thus: In organizations we don't deal with problems—we deal with "messes of problems

Messes of Problems

"Effective managers do not solve problems.
They dissolve messes."

—Dr. Russell L. Ackoff,
Chairman, Interact

PRIMARY SYSTEMS THINKING QUESTIONS

PRIMARY SYSTEMS QUESTIONS = STRATEGIC THINKING

I. Preconditions

Precondition #1 – What System?

What entity/system or 'collision of systems' are we dealing with?

Precondition #2 – What Levels?

Within our identified system, what level(s) of the system are we trying to change and what is our purpose/desired outcome?

II. Systems Questions

Systems Question #1 – Desired Outcomes

What are the desired outcomes?

Systems Question #2 - Feedback

And, how will I know I've achieved it? (i.e., feedback loop of outcome measures)

Systems Question #3 - Environment

What will be changing in the environment in the future that might impact us?

Systems Question #4 – Web of Relationships

What is the relationship of X to Y?

Systems Question #5 – Means or Ends

Are we dealing with means or ends? Corollary: Ask the "five why's".

Systems Question #6 – Booster Shots

What do we need to do to ensure buy in/stay in and perseverance over time (to reverse the entropy)?

Systems Question #7 – Successful Change

What are the new structures and processes we are using to ensure successful change?

Systems Question #8 - Flexibility

What do we centralize (mostly what's) and what should we decentralize (mostly how) at the same time?

Systems Question #9 – Root Causes

What are the root causes?

Systems Question #10 - Simplicity

How can we go from complexity to simplicity and from consistency to flexibility in the solution we devise?

The Foundation Tool and Question

What is it that I contribute to the problem and can change to be a positive and proactive leader on this?

The Ultimate Tool and Question: Helicopter View

What is our common superordinate goal here?

Paradigm Shift Question: Backwards Thinking

What today is impossible to do, but if it could be done, would fundamentally change what we do?

Multiple Goals Question: What are the multiple goals for this project (WIIFM)?

ebsst2.pmd

1420 Monitor Road • San Diego • California • 92110-1545 • (619) 275-6528 • Fax (619) 275-0324

Analytic Thinking Examples

1. Is it either "X" or "Y"?
2. Which one is it?
3. Which is the most important, the best, etc?
4. What's the problem?

The assumption behind these questions never gets asked. (It's an unconscious, analytical, reductionistic mind set and thought process.)

Relationships of X and Y (two parts)
(in a System)

Are they:

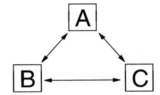

1. Independent?
2. One-way Linear/Dependent (X ➜ Y)
   –or–
3. Interdependent (mutual effect)?

Cause and Effect vs. Root Causes

Cause and effect are not closely related in time and space.

Most of us assume that cause and effect occur close together. That makes it hard to find the root causes that effects—like sagging profits or drug abuse—indicate exist.

The first step in learning how to view reality systemically is to dispense with simple cause-and-effect thinking and learn to see that often we are at the root of our own problems, not external adversaries or events.

Source: *The Fifth Discipline,* Peter M. Senge.

1420 Monitor Road • San Diego • California • 92110-1545 • (619) 275-6528 • Fax (619) 275-0324

ANALYTIC VS. SYSTEMS THINKING
(Strategic Consistency yet Operational Flexibility)

(Outside – In – Outside Again: Both Are Then Useful)

 Success Key: *Organizational Systems Fit, Alignment, and Integrity*

Analytic Thinking (Analysis of Today)	vs.		Systems Thinking (Synthesis for the Future)
1. We/they	vs.	1.	Customers/stakeholders
2. Independent	vs.	2.	Interdependent
3. Activities/tasks/means	and	3.	Outcomes/ends
4. Problem solving	and	4.	Solution seeking
5. Today is fine	vs.	5.	Shared vision of future
6. Units/departments	and	6.	Total organization
7. Silo mentality	vs.	7.	Cross-functional teamwork
8. Closed environment	vs.	8.	Openness and feedback
9. Department goals	and	9.	Shared core strategies
10. Strategic Planning project	vs.	10.	Strategic Management System
11. Hierarchy and controls	and	11.	Serve the customer
12. Not my job	vs.	12.	Communications and collaboration
13. Isolated change	vs.	13.	Systemic change
14. Linear/begin-end	vs.	14.	Circular/repeat cycles
15. Little picture/view	vs.	15.	Big picture/holistic perspective
16. Short-term	and	16.	Long-term
17. Separate issues	vs.	17.	Related issues
18. Symptoms	and	18.	Root causes
19. Isolated Events	and	19.	Patterns/trends
20. Activities/Actions	and	20.	Clear outcome expectations (Goals/Values)
Sum: Parts are Primary	**vs.**		**Whole is Primary**

STOP Using "Analytic Approaches to Systems Problems"

Systems vs. Analytic Thinking

In Systems Thinking — the whole is primary and the parts are secondary
vs.
In Analytic Thinking — the parts are primary and the whole is secondary.

---

ebsst2.pmd

1420 Monitor Road • San Diego • California • 92110-1545 • (619) 275-6528 • Fax (619) 275-0324

RAISE YOUR STRATEGIC I.Q. 50 POINTS

Living systems concepts
are the way the world naturally operates.

AND

To know them makes life easier.

SO

Learn these concepts

AND

Raise your Strategic I.Q. 50 points

DON'T LIVE IN AN ANALYTIC PRISON

"We live and work in an analytic prison.
Working hard within this prison produces
nothing. We cannot remodel the prison, we
must get out of it.

To do this, a transformation is required.
Cooperation between people, companies,
government, countries. There will be joy in
working. Everyone will win."

*– Dr. W. Edwards Deming, April 21, 1992
presentation, The New Economics*

ebsst2.pmd

1420 Monitor Road • San Diego • California • 92110-1545 • (619) 275-6528 • Fax (619) 275-0324

THE SYSTEMS THINKING APPROACH℠
KEY BENEFITS

1. A way of thinking more effectively about any system
   - Its purposes
   - Its environment
   - Its components
2. A framework and way to make sense out of life's complexities – since all living things are systems.
3. A way to learn new things easier as the basic rules stays the same from system to system.
4. A framework for diagnosing, analyzing, problem solving, and decision making of the system. A clearer way to see and understand what is going on in an organization – or in any system. Complex problems become easier to understand, as do the interrelationship of parts and the multiple causes/effects cycles.
5. A way to manage in the complex "systems age," i.e., focusing on the whole, its components, and the *interrelationships* of the components. A better way to integrate new ideas together within the systems context
6. A way to see the big picture as well as the details
7. A view of the long-term and the short-term consequences.
8. A new and better way to create strategies, solve problems, find leverage points, keeping the outcome/vision goal in mind at all times. It unveils points of leverage for change that might otherwise be ignored.
9. A method of understanding the relationship, patterns and themes between issues and events
10. A method for identifying the root causes to a current problem. It engages teams and people in a deeper thought process/analysis and definition of more root causes that provide longer lasting results.
11. It helps get at the deeper structure and relationship/process issues that aren't obvious by the "Quick Fix" mentality.
12. A framework for focusing on the customer and your external environment
13. A forward looking, solution seeking perspective vs. just problem solving today's issues.
14. A common language with a better way to communicate and collaborate

In Summary: A New and Better Orientation to Success in Life and Work

TYPES OF SYSTEMS
(AND MIXTURES OF THESE TOO)

1. **Mechanical Systems** (with Electrical too)—cars, clocks, assembly lines

2. **Electronic Systems** (with Telecommunications too)—PCs, LANs, WANs, supercomputers, INTERNET

3. **Ecological Systems**—21 Regions of North America

4. **Biological Systems**—birds, fish, animals, insects

5. **Human (Living) Systems** (with Social, Organizational too)—individuals, teams, families, organizations, communities

---

Open vs. Closed Systems
More Closed ← Relatively → More Open

Open Systems

Systems can be considered in two ways; closed or open.

While they are difficult to defend in the absolute, the concept of relatively open or relatively closed systems is important.

As system isolated from its environment is called a closed system. One that receives inputs from the environment and/or acts on the environment through outputs is called an open system.

---

ebsst3.pmd

1420 Monitor Road • San Diego • California • 92110-1545 • (619) 275-6528 • Fax (619) 275-0324

The Earth is a Living, Moving System...of Plates

Forty million years ago, India and Australia rode as fellow passengers on board a great tectonic plate steaming slowly northward. But the two travelers have started moving in different directions in recent geologic time, causing the once united Indo-Australian plate to begin splitting apart.

Tectonic plates are large sections of Earth's outer shell, or lithosphere that float on a semi-soft layer of rock in the mantle. Geologists at present recognize a dozen major tectonic plates and several smaller ones. The new findings, if conformed by later studies, would bring the number of major plates to 13.

—*Science News*, August 19, 1995

What else is living/moving about Earth?

- winds/weather
- water/tides
- occupants:
    - plants
    - fish
    - animals
    - birds
    - people

SEVEN LEVELS OF LIVING (OPEN) SYSTEMS

"And the Big Four Systems Levels"   —Kenneth Boulding

SYSTEMS—THE NATURAL ORDER OF THE EARTH

1. **Cell** — the basic unit of life — the smallest unit (system) capable of independent functioning.

2. **Organ** — the systems in our body

3. **Organism** – Individuals

4. **Group** — teams, families

5. **Organization** — firm, community, city, public/private   — *Organizational Focus*

6. **Society** — countries, nations, regions of countries

7. **Supranational System** — continents, earth

8. **Solar System?**

9. **Universe?**

Question: **Are there any other living systems as we know them?**

Question: **Do each of these seven levels constitute a "system"?**
(i.e., sets of interrelated components that [should] work together for the overall objective good of the whole)

Question: **Are systems, then, the natural order of the earth?**

Our organizational focus is usually these four levels (#3, 4, 5, 6) of the Living Systems – and the collisions of these systems with each other, both:

- within each hierarchical level (i.e., 1-to-1), and
- between each hierarchical level (i.e., group/department vs. organization)

LIVING SYSTEMS WITHIN LIVING SYSTEMS

Nested and Interdependent Systems

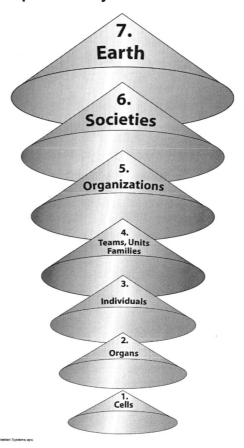

7. Earth

6. Societies

5. Organizations

4. Teams, Units Families

3. Individuals

2. Organs

1. Cells

Nested Systems.eps

Boundaries and Inter-Connectedness
Nothing exists in isolation.
Relationships are everything!

ebsst3.pmd

1420 Monitor Road • San Diego • California • 92110-1545 • (619) 275-6528 • Fax (619) 275-0324

SIX NATURAL RINGS OF REALITY

(FOR ENTERPRISE-WIDE CHANGE)

> "Engineer Success Up Front"
> with Planning for Change
> Level-By-Level

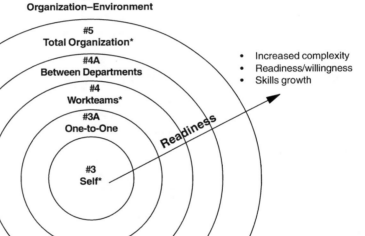

- Increased complexity
- Readiness/willingness
- Skills growth

#5A Organization–Environment
#5 Total Organization*
#4A Between Departments
#4 Workteams*
#3A One-to-One
#3 Self*

Readiness

Note: *Rings 3–4–5 are 3 of the "7 Levels of Living Systems" (individuals – teams – organizations) Rings 3A–4A–5A are "Collisions of Systems" interacting with other systems

Source: Stephen G. Haines, 1980; updated 1988, 1994,1998 and 2003

ebsst3.pmd

1420 Monitor Road • San Diego • California • 92110-1545 • (619) 275-6528 • Fax (619) 275-0324

GENERAL PURPOSES OF WORKING AT EACH RING

Ring #3 Individuals ("Self-Mastery")
- Improve personal competency and effectiveness
- Trustworthiness issues

Ring #3A One-to-One Relationships ("Interpersonal Skills/Effectiveness")
- Improve the interpersonal and working relationships and effectiveness of each individual.
- Trust issues

Ring #4 Workteams/Groups ("Team Empowerment/Effectiveness")
- Improve the effectiveness of the workteam as well as its members.
- Empowerment issues

Ring #4A Intergroups ("Conflict/Horizontal Collaboration")
- Improve the working relationships and business processes between teams/departments horizontally to serve the customer better.
- Horizontal collaboration/integration issues

Ring #5 Total Organization ("Fit"/Strategic Plan)
- Improve the organization's systems, structures and processes to better achieve its business results and potential; and develop its capacity to provide and adaptive system of change and response to a changing environment while pursuing your vision and strategic plan.
- Alignment issues

Ring #5A Organization-Environment (Alliances)
- Improve the organization's sense of direction, response to its' customers and proactive management of its environments/stakeholders by Reinventing Strategic Planning for the 21st Century (Includes Goal #1: Plans; Goal #2: Successful Implementation; and Goal #3: Sustaining Performance).
- Adaptation to the environment issues

Source: *Stephen G. Haines, 2/80; updated 3/88, 7/94 and 6/03*

1420 Monitor Road • San Diego • California • 92110-1545 • (619) 275-6528 • Fax (619) 275-0324

THE CENTRE'S HEAVILY RESEARCHED COMPETENCIES

The Systems Thinking Approach℠

PROVEN BEST PRACTICES RESEARCH

Centering Your Leadership	27 Other Authors
1. Enhancing Self-Mastery	1. 27 out of 27 had a similar item
2. Building Interpersonal Relationships	2. 17 out of 27 had a similar item
	3. 6 out of 27 had a similar item
3. Facilitating Empowered Teams	4. 3 out of 27 had a similar item
4. Collaborating Across Functions	5. 13 out of 27 had a similar item
5. Integrating Organizational Outcomes	6. 9 out of 27 had a similar item
6. Creating Strategic Alliances	

Note: None had all 6 competencies.
- Only 3 had four competencies
- Only 4 had three competencies

The Centre does not do basic research. We do action research as well as summarize and synthesize the research of others.

We are translators and interpreters of Best Practices Research.

Management as a Profession

Managers generally don't devote the time and energy to skills that are essential for effective leadership management and communication.

What are they?

Why is it a profession?

How do you make this transition?

---

ebsst3.pmd

1420 Monitor Road • San Diego • California • 92110-1545 • (619) 275-6528 • Fax (619) 275-0324

SUCCESSION PLANNING LEVERAGE

It is "Central" to people as a competitive edge

```
┌─────────────────────────┐
│     Strategic Plan      │
│ ──────────────────────  │
│     People Strategy     │
└─────────────────────────┘
              │
              ▼
┌─────────────────────────────────┐
│      Strategic People Plan       │
│   Employee Development Board     │
│ ──────────────────────────────  │
│      Management/HR Roles         │
└─────────────────────────────────┘
              │
              ▼
```

Succession Planning and Management
(level by level - slowly)

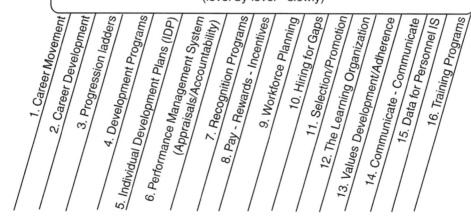

1. Career Movement
2. Career Development
3. Progression ladders
4. Development Programs
5. Individual Development Plans (IDP)
6. Performance Management System (Appraisals/Accountability)
7. Recognition Programs
8. Pay - Rewards - Incentives
9. Workforce Planning
10. Hiring for Gaps
11. Selection/Promotion
12. The Learning Organization
13. Values Development/Adherence
14. Communicate - Communicate
15. Data for Personnel IS
16. Training Programs

Win - Win:

- Employee Satisfaction
- Positive Work Environment
- Organization Depth for future growth
- Stakeholder returns/satisfaction

ebsst3.pmd

1420 Monitor Road • San Diego • California • 92110-1545 • (619) 275-6528 • Fax (619) 275-0324

CULTURE CHANGE: LEVEL-BY-LEVEL

Typical Organizational Culture Levels

The key task is to create one desired culture throughout the total organization at all levels.

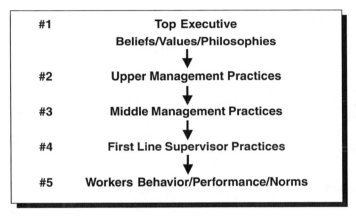

#1	**Top Executive**
	Beliefs/Values/Philosophies
	↓
#2	**Upper Management Practices**
	↓
#3	**Middle Management Practices**
	↓
#4	**First Line Supervisor Practices**
	↓
#5	**Workers Behavior/Performance/Norms**

ORGANIZATIONAL CULTURE DEFINED: The Way We Do Business Around Here

Organizational culture is a set of interrelated beliefs or norms shared by most of the employees of an organization about how one should behave at work and what activities are more important than others.

Assumptions/Philosophy (Our World View)
↓
Personal Values
↓
Organizational Values
↓
Norms of Behavior (i.e., the standards for action)
↓
Individual Behaviors =
↓
Collectively Leads to Our Culture

ebsst3.pmd

1420 Monitor Road • San Diego • California • 92110-1545 • (619) 275-6528 • Fax (619) 275-0324

HOW DOES CHANGE OCCUR?

I. How Does Change Occur?

1. Individually
2. Level
   by
   Level
3. Team
   by
   Team

   • Small units/leadership
   • Cross-functional teams
   • Functional teams
4. Department
   by
   Department

II. Who is Responsible?

1. _____
2. _____
3. _____

_____
_____
_____

4. _____

II. What are the implications for your change effort?

SUB-CULTURES THAT MAY EXIST

1. *Functional* subcultures develop around occupation.

2. *Operating unit* subcultures tend to exist in diversified businesses.

3. *Hierarchical* subcultures can develop at any level of the organization's management.

4. *Social* subcultures may develop within organization's around social activities, such as company softball games.

1420 Monitor Road • San Diego • California • 92110-1545 • (619) 275-6528 • Fax (619) 275-0324

ADVERSARIAL CULTURES
WITHIN AN ORGANIZATION

> It now appears that many of
> the problems of communications,
> productivity, and unionization
> lie primarily in the significantly
> different value systems among
> employee populations.

1.   Managers versus those being managed

– or –

2. Line departments versus staff departments

– or –

3.   Manufacturing versus marketing

– or –

4.   Headquarters versus field

– or –

5.   Division versus division

So, How Do We Achieve Enterprise-Wide Change?

ebsst3.pmd

1420 Monitor Road • San Diego • California • 92110-1545 • (619) 275-6528 • Fax (619) 275-0324

HOW TO DEVELOP A HIGHLY EFFECTIVE ORGANIZATION CULTURE

OR ... LEARNING IS A WAY OF LIFE ... OR ... HOW TO SUCCEED AS AN INDIVIDUAL AND ORGANIZATION?

Question: What are we doing? What should we be doing?

	Levels	Examples	

I.	Individual Level	• technical training
		• managerial training
		• new hire orientation/
		  assimilation
		• job design
		• O.J.T./cross training
			• personal growth
			• individual career
			  development
			• continuing education
			• time management
			• management development

II.	One-to-One Relationships	• process skills • goal setting performance appraisal • boss-subordinate relations	• coaching/counseling • communication skills • influence, power skills
III.	Teams	• staff meetings • team building	• dept. systems & processes • meeting skills

IV.	Inter-Department	• design review teams
		• interdepartmental meetings
		• liaisons
			• integrity mechanisms/task
			  forces
			• conflict resolution
			• interdepartmental team
			  building

V.	Organization-Wide	• communication systems • HR management system • committees • large systems change	• management conferences • cross-sectional task forces • strategic planning

VI.	Organization-Environment Interfaces	• briefings
		• outside seminars
		• trade/professional
		  associations
			• customer contacts
			• customer/service training
			• industry conferences/
			  publications

ebsst3.pmd

1420 Monitor Road • San Diego • California • 92110-1545 • (619) 275-6528 • Fax (619) 275-0324

STRATEGIC MANAGEMENT REALITY CHECK

– CASCADE OF CHANGE –

Talk is cheap. That's apparent from the results of a survey of more than 500 small and midsize companies conducted by the Oechsli Institute. Many of their employees say management's actions don't support the mission statement and that their company's workers don't understand what's expected of them. Worse, 8 out of 10 managers, salespeople, and operations employees say they are not held accountable for their own daily performance.

Percentage that answered yes among. . .	Management	Sales/frontline employees
Does your company have a clear written mission statement? ↓	97%	77%
Is that statement supported by management's actions? ↓	54%	55%
Do all departments, branches, and divisions have specific and measurable goals? ↓	54%	57%
Does every employee understand what is expected in terms of performance? ↓	46%	38%
Are all employees held accountable for daily performance?	21%	22%

Source: Performance Survey, the Oechsli Institute, Greensboro, NC; Reprinted in *INC.*/March 1993.
Research repeated by DDI, Training Magazine, June 2003 (with substantially the same results).

ebsst3.pmd

1420 Monitor Road • San Diego • California • 92110-1545 • (619) 275-6528 • Fax (619) 275-0324

THE CASCADE OF PLANNING

"STRATEGIC CONSISTENCY AND OPERATIONAL FLEXIBILITY"

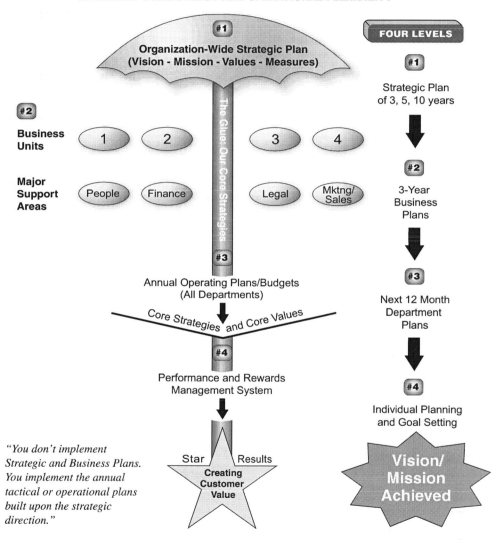

#1 Organization-Wide Strategic Plan
(Vision - Mission - Values - Measures)

FOUR LEVELS

#1 Strategic Plan of 3, 5, 10 years

#2 Business Units: 1, 2, 3, 4

#2 3-Year Business Plans

Major Support Areas: People, Finance, Legal, Mktng/Sales

The Glue: Our Core Strategies

#3 Annual Operating Plans/Budgets (All Departments)

Core Strategies and Core Values

#3 Next 12 Month Department Plans

#4 Performance and Rewards Management System

#4 Individual Planning and Goal Setting

Star / Results
Creating Customer Value

Vision/ Mission Achieved

"You don't implement Strategic and Business Plans. You implement the annual tactical or operational plans built upon the strategic direction."

KEY: Use the Core Strategies as the "Organizing Principle" at all levels.

cascade.eps

ebsst3.pmd

1420 Monitor Road • San Diego • California • 92110-1545 • (619) 275-6528 • Fax (619) 275-0324

TASK

Date: _____
Fiscal Year _____

ANNUAL PLAN FORMAT
(AND FUNCTIONAL/DIVISION/DEPARTMENT PLANS ALSO)

#1 Strategies/Themes/Goals: (What) _____

Yearly Pri #	Strategic Action Items (Actions/Objectives/How?)	Support/Resources Needed	Who Responsible?	Who Else to Involve?	When Done?	Optional How to Measure?	Status

ebsst3.pmd

1420 Monitor Road • San Diego • California • 92110-1545 • (619) 275-6528 • Fax (619) 275-0324

PERFORMANCE APPRAISALS . . .

TIED TO STRATEGIC PLANNING

Performance Appraisals

must be tied to support

#1
Your organization's Core Strategies (i.e., results)
and
#2
Your organization's Core Values (i.e., behaviors)
and
#3
Your own learning and growth (i.e., career development)
(If you are serious about your Strategic Plan)

— **Result: A Four Page Performance Management/Appraisal Form** —

❶

Cover Sheet
Summary
Evaluation

❷

Results	
Strategies	Plan/Actual
1.	
2.	
3.	
4.	
5.	

❸

Values	
Values	Plan/Actual
1.	
2.	
3.	
4.	

❹

Career Development	
Objectives	Action Plan
1. **X** :	
2. **Y** :	
3. **Z** :	

ebsst3.pmd

Page EBSST-82

1420 Monitor Road • San Diego • California • 92110-1545 • (619) 275-6528 • Fax (619) 275-0324

STRATEGIC-ORIENTED ORGANIZATION

Some of the attributes you can expect to find in a systems-oriented organization that might not exist in a more hierarchical one include:

- A shared vision and values of the overall organization's future and culture.
- Better cross-functional communication and cooperation to serve the customer.
- Teamwork within and across functions.
- Cross-functional task forces and project teams/empowerment and self-initiative towards the overall organizational mission.
- Integrity of the various parts and departments of the organization fitting and working together for the good of the whole.
- An alignment of work processes horizontally across the organization that meet the needs of the external customers (and ties in suppliers).
- Focus on system-wide core strategies rather than functional or department goals or individual KRAs.
- Fewer levels of hierarchy and management; greater operational flexibility and empowerment.
- Lower territorial orientation and more job movement across functions.
- Development of management and leadership skills and practices to collaborate with, influence, coach and facilitate others rather than control/power orientation.

ENTERPRISE-WIDE CHANGE

An organization is a system — a complex network of inputs, processes, outputs and feedback from suppliers, employees, and customers.

Management therefore needs a set of concepts and tools for wiring and aligning those components together, with the integrity needed for improving quality and service, reducing time and costs, and implementing strategies.

ebsst4.pmd

THE CENTRE'S STRATEGIC MANAGEMENT CORE TECHNOLOGIES

We use The Systems Thinking Approach[SM] for our Business as a consistent technology, that is the natural way all living/human systems operate on Earth.

I. External Marketplace (Strategic Planning/Positioning)

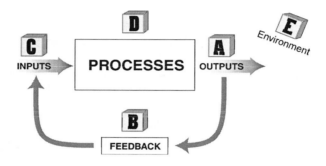

II. Internal Workings (Enterprise-Wide Change)

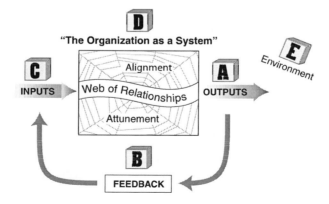

ebstl4.pmd

1420 Monitor Road • San Diego • California • 92110-1545 • (619) 275-6528 • Fax (619) 275-0324

STRATEGIC THINKING FRAMEWORK: SIMPLICITY

MANY USES OF THE FIVE PHASES OF STRATEGIC THINKING AND THE SYSTEMS THINKING APPROACH[SM]

Five Phases of Strategic and Systems Thinking:

A	"Creating Your Ideal Future" (Output)
B	"Measurements of Success" (Feedback Loop)
C	"Converting Strategies to Operations" (The Input to Action)
D	"Successful Implementation" (Throughput/Actions)

Plus | E | Environmental Scanning

Uses:

1. **Comprehensive Strategic Plan**: To do a comprehensive strategic planning process for an entire organization —10-16 days offsite; full steps 1-9, yet tailored to the organization

2. **Strategic Planning Quick**: To conduct a shortened and less comprehensive version of strategic planning for an entire organization — 5 days offsite; skip KSMs

3. **Business/Functional Strategic Planning**: To conduct a shortened 3-year business planning process for a line business unit or major support function/section/program (i.e., element of the larger organization) — 5-10 days, depending on if #1 above is first accomplished

4. **Micro Strategic Planning**: To develop a strategic plan for a small organization or business — 2 days offsite; do the rest without meetings

5. **Strategic Change**: To develop an overall plan for a major project/task force (i.e., TQM, service, business process reengineering, empowerment, partnerships and teamwork, technology, etc.)

6. **Strategic Life Plan**: To conduct a personal (person, family, couple) life plan.

7. **Creating Customer Value**: To create improved value delivered to your customers.

8. **Strategic Human Resource Management**: To create "the *people edge*" in your organization.

9. **Leadership Development System**: To enhance your leadership roles and competencies as a competitive business edge.

10. **A Model of an "Organizational As A System"**: To systematically implement any change effort and to dramatically increase your probability of Business Excellence and Superior Results.

11. **Team Effectiveness**: To comprehensively focus on all aspects of teams to dramatically enhance their outcomes and effectiveness.

12. **Creating the Learning Organization:** Through the Systems Thinking framework and concepts, including environmental scanning, regular feedback and clarity of outcomes.

ebsst4.pmd

1420 Monitor Road • San Diego • California • 92110-1545 • (619) 275-6528 • Fax (619) 275-0324

"STRATEGIC THINKING" FRAMEWORK (cont'd)

13. **GoInnovate!:** A system for swift and continuous innovation to generate wealth (another Centre State-of-the-Art Systems Thinking Approach℠ and it's application to Innovation and Change).

14. **ERP Installations:** Enterprise-wide Resource Planning systems

15. **Reorganizations and re-designs of organizations**

16. **Mergers and Acquisitions**

17. **Cultural change based on organizational values**

18. **Innovation as a specific Cultural Change:** 21st Century need for flexibility, adaptability, and agility as key success values and variables.

19. **Major IT/Telecommunications changes**

20. **Headquarters or Regional Relocations**

21. **Becoming more Customer or Market focused**

22. **Major new product development and rollout**

23. **Large Scale changes such as TQM, Six Sigma, Reengineering**

24. **Empowerment Culture**

1420 Monitor Road • San Diego • California • 92110-1545 • (619) 275-6528 • Fax (619) 275-0324

STRATEGIC SOLUTIONS vs. PROBLEM SOLVING

"Put your discourse into some frame." — William Shakespeare

Phases   **Sequence**

| C | 1. | **Problem Identification**— root causes; not simple cause and effect. |

Now use Systems (and Backwards) Thinking.

Systems Solutions

*2. **Set ideal desired objectives/goals** or multiple outcomes that also solve the root causes (usually a weakness in analytic thinking)...
- with quantifiable measures of success
- and considering what's relevant in the environment

| C | *3. | **Brainstorm alternative strategies/actions** to achieve these ideal outcomes/desired solutions. • There's always a third alternative. Find it. |

- Be sure to collect data and facts about the issues.

4. **Develop tentative strategies** and integrated action plans.

Double back:

*5. **Troubleshoot** the integrated action plans (a weakness in analytic thinking).
- Include examining your biases/assumptions.
- Include a "Parallel Process" to increase buy-in and ownership.
- Remember about the "relationships" of all parts to each other and the overall objectives...and environmental considerations

Recycle

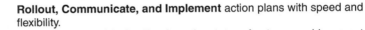

6. **Rollout, Communicate, and Implement** action plans with speed and flexibility.

*7. **Continually provide feedback** on the status of outcome achievement within its environment.

* Systems Steps often missed

USE SYSTEMS THINKING ON THE JOB:

- Help with problem-solving and decision-making.
- Find the root causes of stubborn problems.
- Troubleshoot previously proposed "quick-fix" solutions.
- Increase the range of creativity, alternative discussions and solutions.
- Promote inquiry vs. advocacy, and challenge preconceived ideas. ("Skeptics are our best friends")
- Bring out the validity of multiple perspectives.
- Explore short/long term impacts/consequences of alternatives or newly proposed actions.

Note: Keep the two Employee Handbooks and Job Aid Trifold with you at all times as quick reinforcments.

ebsst4.pmd

1420 Monitor Road • San Diego • California • 92110-1545 • (619) 275-6528 • Fax (619) 275-0324

STRATEGIC THINKING — ONE AGENDA MEETINGS

A-B-C-D-E: The Systems Thinking Approach^{SM}

i.e., "Out of the box thinking" — on a major strategic issue
Make your decisions with "informed intuition"

1. **Keep Asking Questions**

   • What is the wildest idea you can think of in this area? What would it take to do it? What would happen if we did it?

   • What is it you can't do now, but if you could, would fundamentally change your business for the better?

   • Who are the competitors? What are they doing? What is the market data?

   • Take a more holistic—or higher level— systems view (supplier ➔ organization ➔ customer)

2. **Do It As:**

   • Pre-planning–discussion, brainstorming of a topic

   • Post-planning–consensus, debrief

   • When stuck

   • To kick off a topic

   • During the year

3. **Hold One Agenda, One Day Meetings on Key "Nuggets"**

   • With only a very small group of key players on the topic (6-8 maximum)

   • Analyze and discuss the topic in depth—from all angles, with good data

   • Focus on dialogue, discovery and learning; less on planning/documentation

4. **Use the A-B-C-D-E Systems Model** as your discussion framework

   • (see next 2 pages)

   • Work around the circle of E-A-B-C-D-E again and again

1420 Monitor Road • San Diego • California • 92110-1545 • (619) 275-6528 • Fax (619) 275-0324

SYSTEMS THINKING APPROACH^{SM}
A CHARTER/TASK FORCE PROJECT FOR:

"Begin with the end in mind."
— *Steven Covey*

"Problems created at one level of thinking can't be solved
at that same level of thinking."
— *Albert Einstein*

A Desired Outcomes:	**B** Key Success Measures
1.	1.
2.	2.
3.	3.

C Charter/Task Force Details   **E** Environmental Scan

1. Products and Services

2. Primary Customers

3. Marketplace/Revenue Impact

4. Competitor Implications

5. People Implications

6. Return on Investment

D Charter/Task Force Time Line for Implementation:

ebsst4.pmd

1420 Monitor Road • San Diego • California • 92110-1545 • (619) 275-6528 • Fax (619) 275-0324

STRATEGIC THINKING – ABCs TEMPLATE
"The Simplicity of Systems Thinking"

(Name of the System - Issue - Problem - Project - Change Effort, etc.)

A — **Desired Outcomes - #1 Systems Question:** *Where do we want to be?*

Outputs

E — **Future Environmental Scan:** *What will be changing in your future environment that will affect you? (See details on other side)*

D — **System Throughput/Processes:** *How do we get there (close the gap from C → A)?*

CORE STRATEGIES: TOP PRIORITY ACTIONS:

B — **Feedback Loop / Measurements:** *How will we know when we get there?*

C — **Current State Assessments:** *Where Are We Now (SWOT)?*

Inputs

Strengths

Weaknesses

Opportunities

Threats

ebstl4.pmd

1420 Monitor Road • San Diego • California • 92110-1545 • (619) 275-6528 • Fax (619) 275-0324

FUTURE ENVIRONMENTAL (SKEPTIC) SCANNING/TRENDS

What are the 5-10 environmental trends – projections – opportunities – threats facing you over the life of your Plan?

S Socio-Demographics (People/Society)

K Competition / Substitutes:

E Economics:

E Ecology:

P Political / Regulatory:

T Technical:

I Industry / Suppliers:

C Customer / Citizens:

ebsst4.pmd

1420 Monitor Road • San Diego • California • 92110-1545 • (619) 275-6528 • Fax (619) 275-0324

THE INTERDEPENDENCE PARADIGM

*"We are all **interdependent** with each other."*

We all know that we are a part of a vast interrelated whole earth/universe—ever since the astronaut pictures of earth from space.

So why don't we focus on the interrelatedness of:

- our environment (everything outside of us)
- our relationships with all of our environment
- desired outcomes, visions, purposes
- sharing/agreeing on these visions
- gaining feedback on this vision and my part in it on a continuing and regular basis

---

Systems and Subsystems

—Dick Beckhard

A company is a system with many subsystems, all of which are interconnected.

Thinking in systems terms means being aware of the web of interrelationships that exist between the parts vs. being aware just of the parts themselves.

---

ebstl4.pmd

ORGANIZATION AS A SYSTEMS MODEL

ORGANIZATIONAL PIECES DEFINED:

What are the names of the parts/elements of any organization? List them — Brainstorm:

1.	16.
2.	17.
3.	18.
4.	19.
5.	20.
6.	21.
7.	22.
8.	23.
9.	24.
10.	25.
11.	26.
12.	27.
13.	28.
14.	29.
15.	30.

THE ORGANIZATION AS A SYSTEM

Instructions: Build your own model.

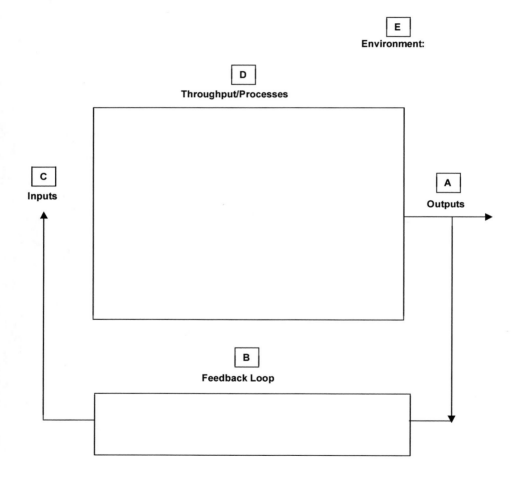

1420 Monitor Road • San Diego • California • 92110-1545 • (619) 275-6528 • Fax (619) 275-0324

ORGANIZATIONAL MODEL
RESEARCH COMPARISONS

(Organization as a Systems Model vs. 13 Other Popular Models)

Organization as a System Model			13 Other Models	
E	1.	Environment	1.	7 out of 13 had a similar item
A	2.	Outputs	2.	8 out of 13 had a similar item
	3.	Values	3.	2 out of 13 had a similar item
	4.	Customer	4.	4 out of 13 mention the customer
	5.	Systems Model	5.	8 out of 13 had a similar item/philosophy
B	6.	Feedback	6.	1 out of 13 had a similar item
C	7.	Strategic Planning (Strategies)	7.	4 out of 13 had a similar item
D_1	8.	Business Processes (Quality/Service)	8.	10 out of 13 had a similar item
	9.	Resources/Technology	9.	10 out of 13 had a similar item; 2 out of 13 included technology
	10.	Organization Redesign	10.	10 out of 13 had a similar item
	11.	Teams	11.	4 out of 13 had a similar item
D_2	12.	Leadership/Management Skills	12.	9 out of 13 had a similar item
	13.	HR/Rewards Systems	13.	8 out of 13 had a similar item
	14.	Culture	14.	6 out of 13 had a similar item
	15.	Strategic Communications	15.	4 out of 13 had a similar item
D_3	16.	Strategic Change Management Process	16.	1 out of 13 had a similar item

ebsst4.pmd

1420 Monitor Road • San Diego • California • 92110-1545 • (619) 275-6528 • Fax (619) 275-0324

WATERTIGHT INTEGRITY

Business Excellence Architecture

(Systems Fit, Alignment, Attunement and Watertight Integrity)

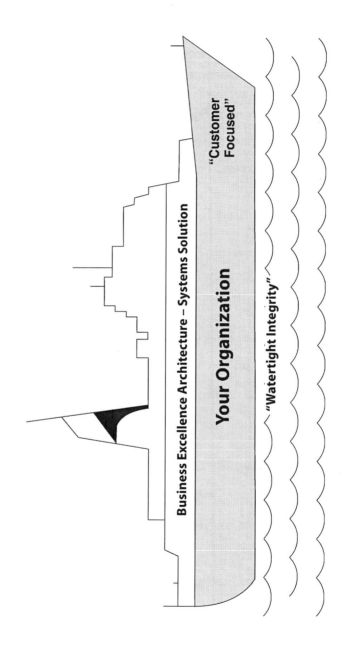

Business Excellence Architecture – Systems Solution

Your Organization

"Customer Focused"

"Watertight Integrity"

ebstl4.pmd

1420 Monitor Road • San Diego • California • 92110-1545 • (619) 275-6528 • Fax (619) 275-0324

STRATEGIC BUSINESS DESIGN (SBD)

> It is no longer centralized vs. decentralized
>
> but
>
> strategic consistency **and** operational flexibility

- **Question:** How do you design your business, leadership, organization, processes and people practices to support your Ideal Future Positioning and core strategies?
- **Answer:** With an integrated and holistic Strategic Business Design for your entire organization to maximize its synergy towards your vision (i.e., **watertight integrity** of design)

(See the Centre's "Organization as a System" Model and associated High Performance Survey for a holistic and integrated example)

Some Topics of a Strategic Business Design:

1. Shared visions/values	and	shared strategies
2. Shared values	and	strong culture
3. Strategies	and	tactics
4. Formal structure	and	formal design
5. Strategic consistency	and	operational flexibility
6. Centralization	and	decentralization
7. Job descriptions	and	roles/responsibilities
8. Policies and procedures	and	accountability
9. Functions	and	business processes
10. Compensation	and	rewards/recognition
11. Full time employees	and	part-time/contract employees
12. Positioning/core competencies	and	outsourcing/strategic alliances
13. Product-based	and	customer-focused

> **Mission → Strategy → Structure (or now "Strategic Business Design")**

BUSINESS EXCELLENCE ARCHITECTURE

THE SYSTEMS THINKING APPROACH℠ TO CREATING YOUR COMPETITIVE BUSINESS ADVANTAGE

D Choice · Service · **CREATING CUSTOMER VALUE** #8 · Responsive · Cost · Quality

B Quadruple Bottom Line Results
- Customers
- Employees
- Shareholders
- Society

E FUTURE ENVIRONMENTAL SCAN

A RESULTS

#2 REINVENTING STRATEGIC PLANNING

#3 LEADING ENTERPRISE-WIDE CHANGE

#7 ALIGNING DELIVERY

#1 BUILDING A CULTURE OF PERFORMANCE EXCELLENCE

#4 CREATING THE PEOPLE EDGE

#6 BECOMING CUSTOMER FOCUSED

#5 ACHIEVING LEADERSHIP EXCELLENCE

"STRATEGIC BUSINESS DESIGN" ·

· "WATERTIGHT - AIRTIGHT INTEGRITY" ·

C BEST PRACTICES ASSESSMENTS

BEA-B.eps

ebstl4.pmd

1420 Monitor Road • San Diego • California • 92110-1545 • (619) 275-6528 • Fax (619) 275-0324

ASSESSMENT vs. THE CENTRE'S BUSINESS EXCELLENCE ARCHITECTURE

Instructions:

1. Please list each module's key strengths and weaknesses.
2. Then score each module (Put an X - Low 1 to 6 High).
3. Connect the scores with a straight line.

Name of Organization _____

Date _____

STRENGTHS

WEAKNESSES

1. Building a Culture of Performance Excellence	HIGH 6 · 5 · 4 · 3 · 2 · 1 LOW
2. Reinventing Strategic Planning	HIGH 6 · 5 · 4 · 3 · 2 · 1 LOW
3. Leading Strategic Change & Innovation	HIGH 6 · 5 · 4 · 3 · 2 · 1 LOW
4. Creating the People Edge	HIGH 6 · 5 · 4 · 3 · 2 · 1 LOW
5. Achieving Leadership Excellence	HIGH 6 · 5 · 4 · 3 · 2 · 1 LOW
6. Becoming Customer-Focused	HIGH 6 · 5 · 4 · 3 · 2 · 1 LOW
7. Aligning Delivery	HIGH 6 · 5 · 4 · 3 · 2 · 1 LOW

ebsst4.pmd

Assessment.eps

1420 Monitor Road • San Diego • California • 92110-1545 • (619) 275-6528 • Fax (619) 275-0324

#1 Use: Business Excellence Architecture: Assessment Summary

Based on the past, which 1-3 items of all the components of the Business Excellence Architecture System Model is your organization likely to fail to implement successfully? (i.e., "The best predictor of future performance is past performance.")

#	Components most likely to fail to be implemented	Result of the failure	Actions to take to counter this

ebstl4.pmd

1420 Monitor Road • San Diego • California • 92110-1545 • (619) 275-6528 • Fax (619) 275-0324

ORGANIZATION ASSESSMENT – STRUCTURED INTERVIEWS – GAP ANALYSIS

instructions: List the event/issue you want to explore and resolve:

WHAT - SO WHAT - NOW WHAT

I.   Beginning Questions:

|A| 1. **What** are your Goals? Mission?

(+) 2. **What helps** you achieve these goals?

(–) 3. **What hinders** you from accomplishing more?

II.   Follow-up root Cause/Cause Effect "Chain" Questions

1. **So what?** (is the result/outcome–or lack thereof if I do nothing different) ➔ |A|

2. **Why?** (does it happen/inputs/root causes) |C| ←

3. **Now what ?** (are you going to do differently)

Assessment Form

2. Why? |C| ➔	List the Issue ➔	1. So What? |A|

Your Model: **"What you look at, is what you see."**
(and Theory)   (Weisbord's "First law of snapshooting)

What you look for, is what you find

What theory you use determines what you look for.

---

ebsst4.pmd

1420 Monitor Road • San Diego • California • 92110-1545 • (619) 275-6528 • Fax (619) 275-0324

"STRATEGIC CHANGE IMPACT EXERCISE"

#2 Use: Organization Design for Action Planning

CREATING A HIGH PERFORMANCE ORGANIZATION
(Using the A–B–C–D–E Phases and the "Business Excellence Architecture" Model)

What components of your organization will/should be impacted by the major change/strategy you propose? Which change/strategy?: _____

Which Components are Impacted and How?	Action Needed/Implications
Phase E Environment 1. _____ Environmental Scanning System 2. _____ Key Environmental Stakeholders (List): _____ _____	
Future Environmental Trends/Scan: 3. _____ S = Socio-demographics 4. _____ K = Competition 5. _____ E = Economics 6. _____ E = Natural Environment 7. _____ P = Political/Regulatory 8. _____ T = Technology 9. _____ I = Industry 10. _____ C = Customers	
Phase A **Module #8—Creating Customer** **Value (Quadruple Bottom Line):** 1. _____ Customer Satisfaction 2. _____ Employee Satisfaction 3. _____ Shareholder Satisfaction 4. _____ Community Satisfaction **Customer Positioning Choices:** 5. _____ Quality Services 6. _____ Quality Products 7. _____ Customer Service (Feelings) 8. _____ Customer Choices 9. _____ Lower Cost Products/Services 10. _____ Speed/Responsiveness/ Convenience	

ebstl4.pmd

continued

1420 Monitor Road • San Diego • California • 92110-1545 • (619) 275-6528 • Fax (619) 275-0324

STRATEGIC CHANGE IMPACT EXERCISE

Which Components are Impacted and How?	Action Needed/Implications?
Module #2—Reinventing Strategic Planning:	
1. _____ Vision	
2. _____ Mission	
3. _____ Organizational Values	
4. _____ Organizational Positioning	
5. _____ Organizational Identity/Image (Brand)	
6. _____ Strategic Business Units	
7. _____ Annual Operating Priorities	
8. _____ Annual Department Plans	
9. _____ Operating Budgets	
10. _____ Capital Budgets	
11. _____ Financing/Banks/Investors	
12. _____ Annual Strategic Review (& Update)	
Phase B	
13. _____ Key Success Measures— Outcome Measures (List): _____ _____ _____	
14. _____ Cascade of metrics to all Management levels	
Phase C	
15. _____ Other Core Strategies (List): _____ _____ _____ _____	

ebsst4.pmd

1420 Monitor Road • San Diego • California • 92110-1545 • (619) 275-6528 • Fax (619) 275-0324

STRATEGIC CHANGE IMPACT EXERCISE

Which Components are Impacted and How?	Action Needed/Implications?
Phase D **Module #1—Culture of Performance Excellence: The Foundation:**	
16. _____ Systems Thinking Language/Skills	
17. _____ Org'n as a Learning Org'n	
18. _____ Innovation & Creativity Language/ Skills	
19. _____ Adult Learning Theory (Experiential Learning)	
20. _____ Group Facilitation	
21. _____ Fact-based Decision-making	
Module #3—Leading Strategic Change:	
22. _____ Change Management Structures	
23. _____ Team Development	
24. _____ Strategic Business Design	
25. _____ Strategic Communication Processes	
26. _____ Empowerment	
27. _____ Key Internal Stakeholders (List): _____ _____ _____	
28. _____ Change Management Plans/ Processes	
Module #4—Attunement with People's Hearts:	
29. _____ Job Design/Definition	
30. _____ Staffing Levels (Recruitment/ Downsizing/Selection)	
31. _____ Performance Appraisal	
32. _____ Rewards System (Pay/Non-Pay)	

ebstl4.pmd

1420 Monitor Road • San Diego • California • 92110-1545 • (619) 275-6528 • Fax (619) 275-0324

STRATEGIC CHANGE IMPACT EXERCISE

Which Components are Impacted and How?	Action Needed/Implications?
Module #5—Leadership Development System:	
32. _____ Succession Planning for Executives & Management	
33. _____ Succession Planning for Key Other Jobs/Roles	
34. _____ Leadership Development System	
Training & Development:	
35. _____ Executives	
36. _____ Management/Supervisors	
37. _____ Sales & Marketing	
38. _____ Workforce Training	
Module #6—Becoming Customer Focused:	
39. _____ Strategic Marketing/Sales Planning	
40. _____ Market Research/Customer Needs	
41. _____ Sales Management	
42. _____ Marketing Management	
Module #7: Alignment of Delivery:	
43. _____ Daily Operating Tasks	
44. _____ Continuous Process Improvement/ Waste Elimination	
45. _____ Business Processes Re-engineered	
46. _____ Simplify Policies & Procedures	
47. _____ Enterprise-Wide Technology	
48. _____ Supply-Chain Management	
49. _____ Facilities & Equipment	
50. _____ Cross-Department Knowledge Transfer	

ebsst4.pmd

1420 Monitor Road • San Diego • California • 92110-1545 • (619) 275-6528 • Fax (619) 275-0324

WHAT'S THE USE OF THE
BUSINESS EXCELLENCE ARCHITECTURE MODEL?

1. A template, model, or diagnostic tool.
2. A framework for thinking and analyzing our organization (or department).
3. Questions to ask as I/we make decisions to change items/tasks in the organization (i.e., implement our Strategic Plan).
4. A common framework for thinking, communicating, and working together to change parts of our organization and achieve our Vision.
5. An increased awareness, sensitivity, and understanding of how an organization works and how the parts should fit together in support of our Vision/customers.
6. A tool to diagnose the status of our effectiveness in both achieving our organization's "fit, alignment, and integrity" to our vision and to our desired culture.
7. Exquisite simplicity, macro model; use it to get a handle on organizational changes.
8. To eliminate biases.
9. To give you a focus through organizational complexity.
10. Bird's eye view/framework to look at the overall organization.
    - multiple cause and effect
    - a balanced way to cover the waterfront
11. Help narrow in on areas needing work.
    - set priorities for work
    - clear linkages/interdependence to other functions, tasks
12. Road map—not get lost in the organization complexity.
    - know where you are and how to navigate to success
    - 21st century road map vs. 1700s map
13. Diagnose problems/solutions in organizations and how one thing affects all others to increase chance of success.
14. To explain, teach executives/managers how to manage/lead strategic planning/ strategic change.
    - readiness check
15. A way to guide any large scale change and to improve individual/team performance and links to the vision/values, direction.
16. To have more confidence in your implementation.
17. To learn how multi-causes have multi-effects.
    - simple cause/effect is obsolete
18. Help ensure strategies/actions are based on a systems diagnosis.

1420 Monitor Road • San Diego • California • 92110-1545 • (619) 275-6528 • Fax (619) 275-0324

HISTORICAL AND NATURAL CYCLES OF CHANGE AND LEARNING

1. **The Environment (Earth)**
   - Santa Ana's, winds
   - El Nino, tides, ocean
   - Volcanoes
   - Earthquakes, plate movement
   - Seasons
   - Moon
   - Day/night
   - Whale/bird migration

2. **Economics**
   - Bull/bear markets
   - K-wave (long wave – Nikolai Kondratieff, 1926)
   - Recessions, depressions
   - Profit taking
   - Inflation

3. **Civilizations**
   - Inca/Aztec/Myan empires
   - British empire
   - French empire
   - Spanish empire
   - Japanese dynasties
   - Chinese dynasties
   - African empire
   - Roman empire
   - Greek empire
   - Persian empire
   - USSR
   - Current Western civilization

4. **Ages**
   - Hunting, gathering, migratory
   - Agriculture
   - Industrial
   - Information
   - Systems (biogenetics–2000?)

5. **Industries**
   - Start up
   - High growth
   - Maturity
   - Decline
   - Renewal

6. **Travel**
   - Walk
   - Animals
   - Row boats, canoes
   - Carts, wheels
   - Automobile
   - Bus, ships
   - Mass Transit
   - Airplanes, flight

7. **Flight**
   - Balloon
   - Wright Brothers – biplanes
   - Single wing propeller
   - Jet planes
   - Concorde plane
   - Satellites, rockets
   - Space shuttles

8. **Life**
   - birth/death
   - food cycle
   - food chain
   - war/peace
   - growth/decline

ebsst5.pmd

1420 Monitor Road • San Diego • California • 92110-1545 • (619) 275-6528 • Fax (619) 275-0324

THE ROLLERCOASTER OF CHANGE℠

CHAOS AND COMPLEXITY – AND STRATEGIC THINKING

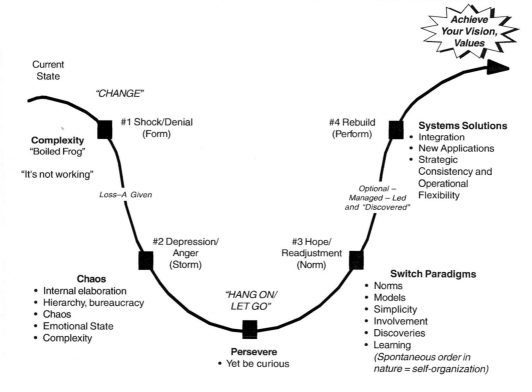

"The natural order of life consists of cycles upon cycles."

"Discovery"
"Discovery consists in seeing what everyone else has seen
and thinking what no one else has thought."
—*Albert Szent-Gyorgi*

Chaos and Complexity
Chaos and complexity are a normal and natural part of the process of change
—of discovering new ways of being and achieving new visions.

---

ebsst5.pmd

1420 Monitor Road • San Diego • California • 92110-1545 • (619) 275-6528 • Fax (619) 275-0324

ROLLERCOASTER OF CHANGE^{SM}

"Persevere" — The Key to Strategic Change

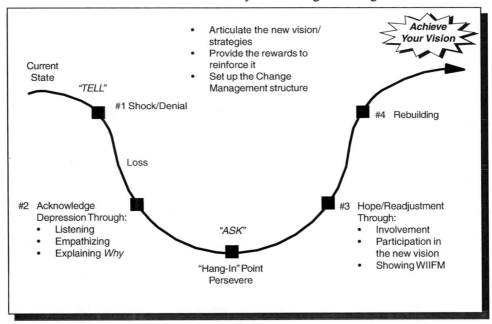

Major Questions

1. Not "if" but "when" will we start to go through shock/depression?
2. How deep is the trough?
3. How long will it take?
4. Will we get up the right (optional) side and rebuild?
5. At what level will we rebuild?
6. How many different rollercoasters will we experience in this change?
7. Are there other changes/rollercoasters occurring?
8. Will we "hang-in" and "persevere" at the midpoint (bottom)? How?
9. How will we deal with normal resistance?
10. How will we create a "critical mass" to support and achieve the change?

ebsst5.pmd

1420 Monitor Road • San Diego • California • 92110-1545 • (619) 275-6528 • Fax (619) 275-0324

PERSISTENCE . . . HANG IN

"Nothing in the world can take the place of persistence. Talent will not; nothing is more common than unsuccessful men with talent. Genius will not; unrewarded genius is almost a proverb. Education will not; the world is full of educated derelicts. Persistence and determination alone are omnipotent."

Source: Calvin Coolidge

"A basic truth of management — if not of life — is that nearly everything looks like a failure in the middle . . . persistent, consistent execution is unglamourous, time-consuming, and sometimes boring."

Source: Rosabeth Moss Kanter, July 1990

All Change is a Loss Experience

1. **Loss** creates a feeling of depression for most people. One loses preferred modes of attaining and giving affection, handling aggression, dependency needs—all those *familiar routines* which we have evolved and usually taken for granted.

2. **Loss** is a difficult experience to handle, particularly if what one leaves behind is psychologically important.

3. **All loss** must be mourned and the attendant feelings disgorged if a restitution process is to operate effectively.

4. **Most** organization change flounders because the experience of loss is not taken into account. *To undertake successful organizational change, an executive must anticipate and provide the means of working through that loss and all four phases of it.*

Adapted from Harry Levinson, *Psychological Man*

---

ebsst5.pmd

1420 Monitor Road • San Diego • California • 92110-1545 • (619) 275-6528 • Fax (619) 275-0324

ENTERPRISE-WIDE CHANGE AND EXCELLENCE

THE FIVE CHOICES OF CHANGE AND LEVELS OF EXCELLENCE

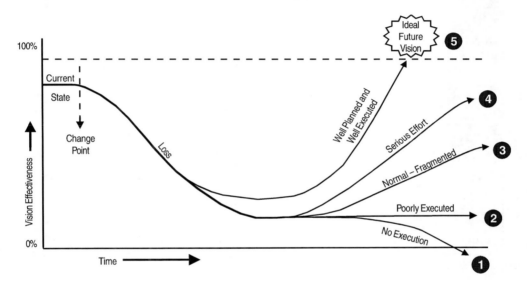

Which will you be?

_____ **1** **Incompetence**—"Going Out of Business"

_____ **2** **Technical** — "Dogged Pursuit of Mediocrity"

_____ **3** **Management** — "Present and Accounted For Only"

_____ **4** **Leadership** — "Making a Serious Effort"

_____ **5** **Visionary Leadership** — "Developing an Art Form"

ebsst5.pmd

1420 Monitor Road • San Diego • California • 92110-1545 • (619) 275-6528 • Fax (619) 275-0324

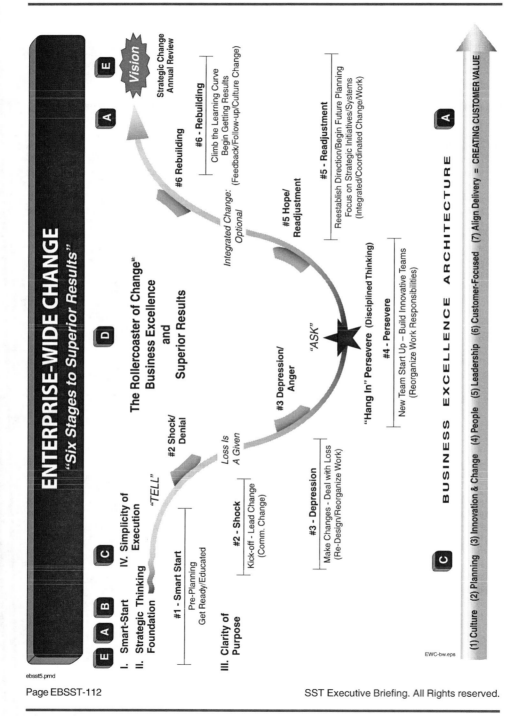

ENTERPRISE-WIDE CHANGE
"Six Stages to Superior Results"

The Rollercoaster of Change℠
Business Excellence and **Superior Results**

I. Smart-Start
II. Strategic Thinking Foundation
III. Clarity of Purpose
IV. Simplicity of Execution

"TELL"

#1 - Smart Start
Pre-Planning
Get Ready/Educated

#2 Shock/Denial

Loss Is A Given

#2 - Shock
Kick-off - Lead Change
(Comm. Change)

#3 Depression/Anger

#3 - Depression
Make Changes - Deal with Loss
(Re-Design/Reorganize Work)

"ASK"

"Hang In" Persevere (Disciplined Thinking)
#4 - Persevere
New Team Start Up – Build Innovative Teams
(Reorganize Work Responsibilities)

Integrated Change: Optional

#5 Hope/Readjustment

#5 - Readjustment
Reestablish Direction/Begin Future Planning
Focus on Strategic Initiatives/Systems
(Integrated/Coordinated Change/Work)

#6 Rebuilding

#6 - Rebuilding
Climb the Learning Curve
Begin Getting Results
(Feedback/Follow-up/Culture Change)

Vision

Strategic Change Annual Review

BUSINESS EXCELLENCE ARCHITECTURE

(1) Culture (2) Planning (3) Innovation & Change (4) People (5) Leadership (6) Customer-Focused (7) Align Delivery = CREATING CUSTOMER VALUE

EWC-bw.eps

ebsst5.pmd

1420 Monitor Road • San Diego • California • 92110-1545 • (619) 275-6528 • Fax (619) 275-0324

STANDARD "KNEE-JERK" SIMPLISTIC IMPLEMENTATION TECHNIQUES

(THAT FAIL)

Question: Which do you do? Check the #.

1. _____ Form a team or committee; hold a meeting.
2. _____ Set up a suggestion/recognition system.
3. _____ Set up a training program(s).
4. _____ Improve communications—videos, policy, newsletter, memos.
5. _____ Define a Vision, Mission, and Values.
6. _____ Improve our performance appraisal form.
7. _____ Empower people.
8. _____ Hire a staff expert/delegate it (i.e., HR, QC, T/D, MIS, Planning)
9. _____ Hold a yearly retreat.
10. _____ Problem solve it: one issue at a time.
11. _____ Cut costs across the board.
12. _____ Have a hiring freeze.
13. _____ Hold someone accountable; punish or terminate him or her.
14. _____ Set up a merit increase; "pay-for-performance" program.
15. _____ Have a flurry of activity (but short-lived)

_____ Total Points

What Else?

16. _____
17. _____
18. _____
19. _____
20. _____

LEVERAGE POINTS IN CHANGE

(WITH SYSTEMS THINKING)

Complex systems are changed

by small interventions

(if in the right place)

Caterpillar to Butterfly Effect

The butterfly effect is this:
Minuscule differences in the
beginning abruptly become
massive differences in the results.

Systems Thinking helps you see patterns in the world
and spot the leverage points that, acted upon,
lead to lasting beneficial changes.

Adaptable and Flexible

It is not the strongest of the species that survive.
Nor the most intelligent,
But the one most responsive to change.

—*Charles Darwin*

ebsst5.pmd

1420 Monitor Road • San Diego • California • 92110-1545 • (619) 275-6528 • Fax (619) 275-0324

CONTENT — PROCESS — STRUCTURE

THE ICEBERG THEORY OF ENTERPRISE-WIDE CHANGE
(To Achieve Your Competitive Business Edge)

Efforts:

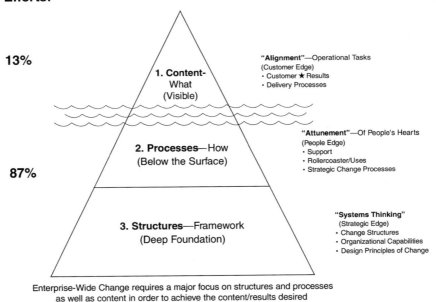

13%

1. **Content**-
   What
   (Visible)

"Alignment"—Operational Tasks
(Customer Edge)
• Customer ★ Results
• Delivery Processes

2. **Processes**—How
(Below the Surface)

"Attunement"—Of People's Hearts
(People Edge)
• Support
• Rollercoaster/Uses
• Strategic Change Processes

87%

3. **Structures**—Framework
(Deep Foundation)

"Systems Thinking"
(Strategic Edge)
• Change Structures
• Organizational Capabilities
• Design Principles of Change

Enterprise-Wide Change requires a major focus on structures and processes
as well as content in order to achieve the content/results desired

Iceberg EBSTL.eps

Content Myopia
is
Our failure to focus on processes and structures
–yet–
Successful change is dependent on processes and structures

ebsst5.pmd

1420 Monitor Road • San Diego • California • 92110-1545 • (619) 275-6528 • Fax (619) 275-0324

TEAM PROCESSES AND STRUCTURES

—Processes— The Way in Which the Team Accomplishes the Work/Tasks	—Structures— Structural Elements of Meetings and Groups
1. Decision-making	Structure is the design or the physical reality. *The third element besides Content and Process includes:*
2. Communication styles	
3. Meetings management	1. Room
4. Leadership styles/expectations	2. Location
5. Conflict management	3. Attendees
6. Performance/results management	4. Purpose
7. Rewards/Recognition management	5. Agenda (beginning – middle – end)
8. Relationship/team maintenance	6. Seating
9. Diagnosing our effectiveness/norms as a team	7. Room Arrangements
	8. Refreshments
10. Giving and receiving feedback	9. Flip Charts
11. Self-disclosure and openness	10. Overheads
12. Encouraging/supporting each other's tasks/priorities	11. Podium
	12. Timeframe
13. Levels of participation/involvement	13. Logistics
14. Goals/roles process determination	14. Roles
15. Climate, tone, respect	15. Breaks
16. Problem solving	16. To Do List
17. Planning process	17. Guidelines/Norms
18. Information sharing	18. Materials
19. Use of time	19. Climate
20. Use of facilitator/recorder	• Open – Trust – Honesty • Fun – Casual – Real • Movement
	20. Appearance/Dress

1420 Monitor Road • San Diego • California • 92110-1545 • (619) 275-6528 • Fax (619) 275-0324

ENTERPRISE-WIDE CHANGE MANAGEMENT

"A MENU" – STRUCTURES AND ROLES

MAIN STRUCTURES – SENIOR LEADERSHIP

1. **Visionary Leadership** — CEO/Senior Executives with **Personal Leadership Plans (PLPs)**
   - For repetitive stump speeches and reinforcement
   - To ensure fit/integration of all parts & people towards the same vision/values
2. **Internal Support Cadre** — Informal/kitchen cabinet
   - For day-to-day coordination of implementation process
   - To ensure the change structures & processes don't lose out to day-to-day
3. **Executive Committee**
   - For weekly meetings and attention
   - To ensure follow-up on the top 15-25 priority yearly actions from the Strategic Plan
4. **Strategic Change Leadership Steering Committee** (formal)—replaces or is the Strategic Planning Team
   - For bimonthly/quarterly follow-up meetings to track, adjust and refine everything (including the Vision)
   - To ensure follow-through via a yearly comprehensive map of implementation
5. **Program Management Office** — Joint internal and external experts
   - For Enterprise-Wide Change requiring management of multiple change processes and projects
   - To ensure "Watertight Integrity" to your Vision, Positioning, and Values (Strategic Business Design)

SUB-STRUCTURES – SUBCOMMITTEES

6. **Strategy Sponsorship/Project Teams**
   - For each core strategy and/or major change effort
   - To ensure achievement of each one; including leadership of what needs to change
7. **Employee Development Board** (Attunement of People's Hearts)
   - For succession – careers – development – core competencies (all levels) – performance management/appraisals
   - To ensure fit with our desired values/culture — and employees as a competitive edge
8. **Technology Steering Committee/Group**
   - For computer — telecommunications — software fit and integration
   - To ensure "system-wide" fit/coordination around information management
9. **Strategic Communications System (and Structures)**
   - For clear two way dialogue and understanding of the Plan/implementation
   - To ensure everyone is heading in the same direction with the same strategies/values
10. **Measurement and Benchmarking Team**
    - For collecting and reporting of Key Success Factors, especially customers, employees, competitors
    - To ensure an outcome/customer-focus at all times
11. **Accountability and Responsibility System**—all levels
    - For clear and focused 3-year business plans and annual department plans that are critiqued, shared and reviewed, as well as individual performance appraisals
    - To ensure a fit, coordination and commitment to the core strategies and annual top priorities
12. **Whole System Participation Team** (can combine with #8)
    - For input and involvement of all key stakeholders before a decision affecting them is made. Includes Parallel Processes, Search Conferences, Annual Management Conferences, etc.
    - To ensure a critical mass in support of the vision and desired changes
13. **Rewards and Recognition Programs** (can combine with #6)
    - For recognizing and paying people for strategic management accomplishments
    - To ensure reinforcement of the Accountability and Responsibilities System
14. **Organization Redesign Team**
    - For studying and recommending what redesign of the organization is needed
    - To ensure synergy of the strategies, structures, processes, policies, values and culture
15. **Environmental Scanning System**
    - For collecting data from the environment (SKEPTIC)
    - To ensure advance awareness of coming changes to the environment

ebsst5.pmd

1420 Monitor Road • San Diego • California • 92110-1545 • (619) 275-6528 • Fax (619) 275-0324

STRATEGIC CHANGE LEADERSHIP
STEERING COMMITTEE (SCLSC)

Ineffectiveness of Hierarchical "Cascade"

Implementation Strategy Alone

The normal "cascade" strategy for implementing change is usually ineffective, because memories remain embedded in the way the organization works after the change. This applies particularly if the change relates to the culture rather than to work practices or systems.

—Dick Beckhard
Changing the Essence

A new way to run your business, giving equal weight to managing desired changes, in addition to the ongoing daily management of the organization.

Purposes
1. To guide and control the implementation of any large scale, organization-wide strategic planning/change efforts undertaken through the "Reinventing Strategic Planning" model.
2. To coordinate any other major performance improvement projects going on in the organization at the same time; to ensure a good fit with the time and energy demands of ongoing daily business activities (i.e., *systems fit, alignment, and integrity*).
3. To establish and institutionalize the three Core Competencies required of every successful organization: 1) Leadership, 2) Strategic Management, and 3) Watertight Integrity.

Criteria for SCLSC Membership and Attendance
1. Senior management leadership teams for today and the future.
2. Formal or Informal organization leaders who are key to implementation.
3. "Core Steering Group Implementation Staff Support Team", including overall change management coordinator, KSM/ESS coordinators, and internal facilitators.
4. Reliable staff who are knowledgeable of the actual Strategic Plan development.
5. Key stakeholders who share your Future Vision, and will actively support it.
6. Senior level, external, master facilitator of Strategic Management (Leadership-Planning-Change)

Committee Meeting Frequency
1. Phase I: Monthly as the process begins.
2. Phase II: Bi-monthly once the process is functioning smoothly.

1420 Monitor Road • San Diego • California • 92110-1545 • (619) 275-6528 • Fax (619) 275-0324

EXECUTIVE/EMPLOYEE DEVELOPMENT BOARD (EDB) CONCEPT

> ## "Invest in Your People First"

The people management practices of any organization should be viewed as a system of people flow from hiring, through their careers, and through retirement and/or termination. See the Centre's copyrighted HR Systems Model and assessment tools. Making this all happen is the responsibility of senior management; usually best done through an "EDB" (Executive/Employee Development Board) focused solely on this framework and "creating people as a competitive business advantage." *(The "People Edge")*

As a Board, this reinforces senior management's responsibility to carry out your "stewardship" responsibilities towards yourselves and the rest of your employees. **The best way to carry this out is to conduct a Strategic "People Edge" Plan to fully define and implement your corporate Strategic Plan's people strategy.**

In essence, this Executive Stewardship Board is responsible for the Human Resource Management flow and continuity. It is executive responsibility to link staffing to business strategy via:

- hiring
- selection (up/lateral)
- succession planning/core competencies
- developmental jobs/experiences
- Leadership Development System
- training: classroom (internal, external)

- organization design/structure
- socio-demographic trends
- employee surveys of satisfaction/360° feedback
- rewards/performance system
- workforce planning

A mechanism/structure of how to achieve management continuity is needed (i.e., a linking pin of Boards):

1. Executive Development Board (EDB)—executive team
2. Management Development Board (MDB)—all department heads/teams
3. Employee Development Committees (EEDC)—all supervisors/section head areas

The desired outcomes include:

Right person — Right job — Right time — Right organization — Right skills!

Sample Monthly Executive Meetings

Week 1	Operational/Business Issues
Week 2	Strategic Planning and Change Process/Status
Week 3	Strategic Change Issues
Week 4	Customer Satisfaction
Week 5	Executive/Employee Development Board (EDB)
(Quarterly)	Staff, promotion, succession, development – HR Executive as secretary to Senior Management

ebsst5.pmd

1420 Monitor Road • San Diego • California • 92110-1545 • (619) 275-6528 • Fax (619) 275-0324

SECTION VI
SUMMARY OF STRATEGIC & SYSTEMS THINKING

DEFINITION

- A comprehensive "system" to lead, manage, and change one's total organization in a conscious, well planned out, and integrated fashion based on our core strategies— and using *proven research that works*— to develop and successfully achieve one's ideal future vision.

- *The new way to run the business* — i.e., "We manage our business in a systematic way based on our strategies."

- The method: interactive and participative.

   "People support what they help create" — a basic truism.

- Is Managed as a complete "Systems Change"

   (with strategic/annual/individual plans, budgets, and measurements)

- Is Successful if it is:
   1. Vision inspired and shared
   2. Mission/customer focused
   3. Values/culturally based
   4. Strategically driven
   5. Outcome/results oriented

- Its hallmark is: *Strategic Consistency Yet Operational Flexibility*
   "Focus – Focus – Focus"

"We Now Need A Strategic Management System"

I need to stress at this point that an effective management system is more than just the sum of the parts . . . it is a set of integrated policies, practices and behaviors.

Sometimes having a good management system is confused with having high-quality employees. This is a mistake—the two are quite different in some important ways: having high-quality employees does not assure an organization of having a sustainable competitive advantage or even a short-term advantage."

—Edward J. Lawler III
The Ultimate Advantage:
Creating the High-Involvement Organization

---

ebsst6.pmd

YEARLY STRATEGIC MANAGEMENT CYCLE
Using The Systems Thinking Approach℠

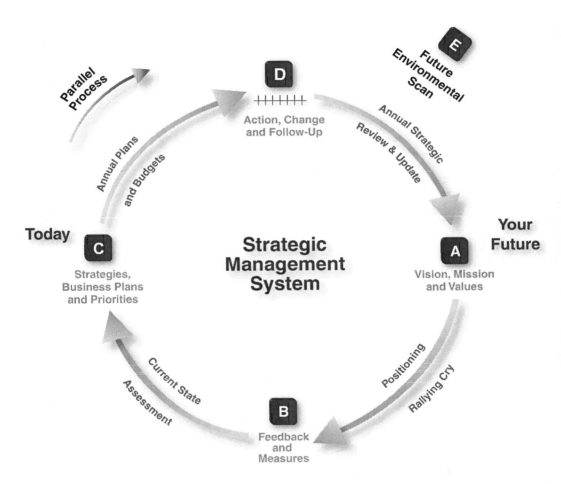

"Thinking Backwards to the Future"

©2003 Centre for Strategic Management® • All rights reserved.
1420 Monitor Road, San Diego, CA 92110
(619) 275-6528 • FAX: (619) 275-0324
Website: www.csmintl.com • Email: info@csmintl.com

YSM-clr.eps
ebsst6.pmd

ANNUAL STRATEGIC REVIEW (AND UPDATE)

Annual Strategic Review (and Update)

(Strategic Management System)

"Similar to a yearly independent financial audit and update"

Goal #1:   Assess the Strategic Management Process and System itself

Goal #2:   Assess the status of the Strategic Plan achievement itself

Resulting in:

1. Updating your Strategic Plan
2. Clarifying your annual planning and strategic budgeting priorities for next year
3. Problem solving any issues raised in either goal
4. Setting in place next year's Annual Plan and Strategic Change Management Process

1420 Monitor Road • San Diego • California • 92110-1545 • (619) 275-6528 • Fax (619) 275-0324

15 KEY BENEFITS OF A
STRATEGIC MANAGEMENT SYSTEM

Which of these benefits are still missing in your organization?

_____ 1. Taking an organization-wide, proactive approach to a changing global world.

_____ 2. Building an executive leadership team that serves as a model of cross-functional or horizontal teamwork.

_____ 3. Having an intense executive development and strategic orientation process on participative management.

_____ 4. Defining focused, quantifiable outcome measures of success.

_____ 5. Making intelligent budgeting decisions.

_____ 6. Clarifying your competitive advantage.

_____ 7. Reducing conflict; empowering the people in the organization.

_____ 8. Providing clear guidelines for day-to-day decision making.

_____ 9. Creating a critical mass for change.

_____ 10. "Singing from the same hymnal" throughout the organization.

_____ 11. Clarifying and simplifying the barrage of management techniques.

_____ 12. Developing and empowering middle managers.

_____ 13. Focusing everyone in the organization on the same overall strategies/framework.

_____ 14. Speeding up implementation of the core strategies.

_____ 15. Providing tangible problem solving and other tools for dealing with the stress of change.

_____ 16. What else?

ebsst6.pmd

1420 Monitor Road • San Diego • California • 92110-1545 • (619) 275-6528 • Fax (619) 275-0324

LANGUAGE MATTERS

"Systems Thinking is a new language and orientation to life"

—Steve Haines

Language matters—that words become commitments and that commitments generate behavior.

In order to transform organizations and to achieve competitive results, we need to tap the oldest deepest roots of human understanding: the way we talk to one another, the words we use, and the commitments we make.

Adapted from: Freedom from Frenzy, Fast Company January 1999

A Language for Learning

Language has a subtle, yet powerful effect on the way we view the world. English, like most other Western languages, is linear—its basic sentence construction, noun-verb-noun translates into a worldview of "A causes B."

This linearity predisposes us to focus on one-way relationships rather than circular or mutually causative ones, where A influences B, and B in turn influences A.

Unfortunately, many of the most vexing problems confronting managers and organizations are caused by a web of tightly interconnected circular relationships.

To enhance our understanding and communication of such problems, **we need a language more naturally suited to the task.**

Elements of the Language. Systems thinking can be thought of as a language for communication about complexities and interdependencies.

—5th Discipline Fieldbook

---

ebsst6.pmd

1420 Monitor Road • San Diego • California • 92110-1545 • (619) 275-6528 • Fax (619) 275-0324

SOME NEW LANGUAGE OF
THE SYSTEMS THINKING APPROACH^{SM}

1. Input – Throughput – Output – Feedback in the Environment (Four Phases of Systems Thinking
2. A–B–C–D (The Four Phases in proper order; A = Output; B = Feedback; C = Input; D = Throughput)—It simplifies the mazes, chaos and messes we see; helps to see the forest and the trees
3. Precondition #1: What entity are we dealing with
4. The #1 and #2 Systems Questions: #1—Outcomes; #2—Feedback
5. #3 Question: ESS (Environmental Scanning System
6. Means/ends
7. Multiple goal seeking
8. Strategic consistency/operational flexibility
9. Backwards thinking
10. The whole is primary, parts secondary
11. Synthesis vs. analysis is a new way of thinking
12. Environment—Living Systems interact in a hierarchy; both always present
13. Messes of problems vs. separate problems
14. Feedback is the breakfast of champions
15. Negative entropy or positive energy continuously into the system — feedback
16. Begin with the end in mind
17. Get outside the 9 Dots
18. Relationships/fit are key — processes are important; not events/units
19. Causes — effects
    - Are circular — not one way
    - Are not related in time/space
20. Simplistic, quick fixes do not work!
21. Causal Loops make things better and better—or worse and worse
22. Seven Levels of Living Systems (especially, #3—individual; #4—team; #5—organization; #6—society; #7—earth
23. KISS Method—reduces complexity, rigidity, bureaucracy and death
24. 5 "Whys"—to reach the true/final outcomes/benefits
25. General Systems Theory

ebsst6.pmd

1420 Monitor Road • San Diego • California • 92110-1545 • (619) 275-6528 • Fax (619) 275-0324

THE SYSTEMS THINKING APPROACH^{SM} TO BUSINESS EXCELLENCE AND SUPERIOR RESULTS

(The new paradigm, language, and approach to today's global complexities)

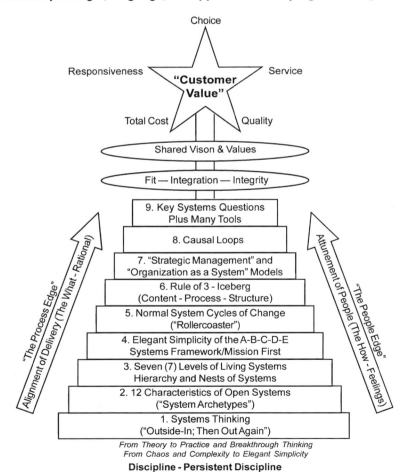

Choice

Responsiveness

"Customer Value"

Service

Total Cost

Quality

Shared Vison & Values

Fit — Integration — Integrity

9. Key Systems Questions Plus Many Tools

8. Causal Loops

7. "Strategic Management" and "Organization as a System" Models

6. Rule of 3 - Iceberg (Content - Process - Structure)

5. Normal System Cycles of Change ("Rollercoaster")

4. Elegant Simplicity of the A-B-C-D-E Systems Framework/Mission First

3. Seven (7) Levels of Living Systems Hierarchy and Nests of Systems

2. 12 Characteristics of Open Systems ("System Archetypes")

1. Systems Thinking ("Outside-In; Then Out Again")

"The Process Edge" Alignment of Delivery (The What - Rational)

Attunement of People (The How - Feelings) "The People Edge"

From Theory to Practice and Breakthrough Thinking
From Chaos and Complexity to Elegant Simplicity

Discipline - Persistent Discipline

ebsst6.pmd

1420 Monitor Road • San Diego • California • 92110-1545 • (619) 275-6528 • Fax (619) 275-0324

SYSTEMS THINKING—A NEW WAY TO THINK

"Think Differently"

Start Thinking About:

1.	The Environment	E	(and opportunities)
2.	The Outcomes	A	(and results)
3.	The Future	A	(and direction)
4.	The Feedback	B	(and learning)
5.	The Goals	B	(and measures)
6.	The Whole Organization	D	(and helicopters @ 5,000 feet)
7.	The Relationships	D	(and patterns)

Stop Thinking About:

1. Issues and Problems

2. Parts and Events

3. Boxes/Silos

4. Single Activities of Change

5. Defensiveness

6. Inputs and Resources

7. Separateness

How we think ... is how we act ... is how we are!

1420 Monitor Road • San Diego • California • 92110-1545 • (619) 275-6528 • Fax (619) 275-0324

SYSTEMS THINKING IS SIMPLICITY

A 5000 Foot Helicopter View

How:

1. Uses natural 'Rule of three' for everything, KISS mind set.

2. Looks at entire system (not piecemeal), end to end solutions.

3. Clarifies your destination first, focuses all activities.

4. Integrates the pieces/functions in pursuit of common goals (outcomes).

5. Recognizes and clarifies relationships between all pieces/functions.

6. Increases teamwork/decreases conflict through coordination/callback and backwards thinking.

7. Flatters the hierarchy/bureaucracy.

8. Builds in 'booster shots' to keep the direction and strategies fresh.

9. Focuses on what is important, the ends, encourages empowerment of means (strategic consistency and operational flexibility).

10. Absorbs the complexity and finds the few key leverage points.

11. Focuses on logic and common sense.

12. "Feedback is the Breakfast of Champions."

13. "People support what they help create."

SIMPLICITY RULE

Let's make a rule that we can't use anything we can't explain in five minutes.

—Bill Cosby

---

ebsst6.pmd

1420 Monitor Road • San Diego • California • 92110-1545 • (619) 275-6528 • Fax (619) 275-0324

MANAGEMENT'S ULTIMATE CHALLENGE

Search for the simplicity on the far side of complexity!

Don't try to make it too simple too soon. First, absorb the complexity of the situation; then start looking for simpler perspectives on it.

Who chooses to take the tough, tangled path when there is a clear alternative? That clean, simple path appeals to me. I am tired and it looks easy. **Here comes simplicity and there goes reality.** There goes complexity and here comes clarity.

But it's not simplicity itself that troubles me, it's our misuse of it. For example, when we offer training solutions in six steps, or when we assess people, stick labels on them, and declare interpersonal issues resolved. Or when our discovery of the latest change model allows us to neglect the real needs of our clients. **Each of those examples uses a simple approach to deny a larger, more complex reality.**

Experience is dehydrated, scooped into a three-ring binder, and the binder is held up as the new truth. And questioning it can be perilous. Look at what we have done with Total Quality, Self-Directed Teams, Process Re-engineering, and The Learning Organization.

The simplicity recipe is: Take a useful perspective on the world, distill its key elements, throw away the rest, build programs around its 14 points, preach them to the multitudes, and wonder why it works less than' a third of the time. That chanting you hear in the background is Deming, Hammer, Weisbord, Senge, and others lamenting **we have lost the art and meaning of their messages in the translation to application.**

The challenge in life is to absorb the messy reality, and deal with it as it is.

—Geoff Bellman
Training & Development, August 1996

ebsst6.pmd

1420 Monitor Road • San Diego • California • 92110-1545 • (619) 275-6528 • Fax (619) 275-0324

Simplicity and Complexity

I wouldn't give a fig for the simplicity this side of complexity

but

I'd give my life for the simplicity on the far side of complexity.

—*Justice Oliver Wendell Holmes*

Simplicity and Genius

Any idiot can simplify by ignoring the complications.

But,

it takes real genius to simplify by including the complications.

—John E. Johnson, TEC Chair
(The Executive Committee)

Simple Answers

For every complex problem there is a simple answer and…it is always wrong.

—*H. L. Menkin*

And Ludwig Von Bertalanffy—the founder of General Systems Theory—is the "genius" and major leader and pioneer of the coming 21st Century systems orientation and simplicity … through our holistic, synergistic and integrated thinking called The Systems Thinking Approach℠

"I think, therefore I am."
—Rene Descartes (1596-1650)

ebsst6.pmd

Page EBSST-130

1420 Monitor Road • San Diego • California • 92110-1545 • (619) 275-6528 • Fax (619) 275-0324

Simplicity is Defined As...

—Bill Jensen

- A common focus

- Clear and concise goals

- Tools to achieve the objectives

- Information readily available to all employees

- Sufficient training and direction to do the job

- All activities linked to serving customer needs

- A tangible and measurable outcome

- Meeting the company's mission/vision

—*Strategy & Leadership*, March/April 1997

- Lack of "politics" and a focus on logic and common sense

—Stephen G. Haines

SOME KEYS TO SIMPLICITY

—Compiled by Steve Haines

1. "Rule of Three" and "Three Times Rule"
2. 80/20 Rule — "Focus, Focus, Focus"
3. The Systems Thinking Approach[SM] (all four concepts)
4. KISS Mindset
5. Single Page Documents
6. Simplicity Rule

> **Simplicity Rule**
> *—P. Crosby*
>
> Let's make a rule that we can't use anything
> I can't explain in five minutes.

7. Flexibility–"Strategic Consistency **and** Operational Flexibility"
8. Fundamentals

> **Fundamentals**
> *—P. Crosby*
>
> We could learn a lot from military training.

9. Thank You cards

> **Simple, Yet Powerful Rewards**
> *—Alan Landers*
>
> 1. Celebrate the moment
> 2. Recognize the effort
> 3. Time with the boss

10. What else?

ebsst6.pmd

1420 Monitor Road • San Diego • California • 92110-1545 • (619) 275-6528 • Fax (619) 275-0324

STRATEGIC MANAGEMENT SYSTEM: IT'S SIMPLE

(Once You Use The Systems Thinking Approach℠)

The Three Foundational Core Competencies of Every Organization on Earth:

1. Have a Shared Direction

A. Develop a Strategic Plan that is Customer-Focused
- with a shared Vision, Values and Core Strategies, pointing to a clear Future Positioning
- develop focused, organization-wide Action Priorities for the next year

B. Develop Buy-in and Stay-in to the Yearly Strategic Management Cycle and Plan
- communicate – communicate – communicate (stump speeches)
- involvement – participative management – and WIFFM

> **Core Competency #2:** *Build an Integrated Strategic Management System*
> *– "Use Systems Thinking – Focus on the Customer"*

2. Develop and Implement/Change to a Consistent Overall Strategic Business Design

A. Conduct a Strategic Business Assessment and Redesign
- to ensure the fit of all policies and parts, people and business processes of the organization – use *Building on the Baldrige*, a Fast Track Best Practices Assessment
- using the overall direction, Strategic Plan and positioning as the criteria

B. Cascade down department work plans, budgets and accountability with Watertight Integrity and Accountability to the Shared Direction
- using the core strategies, action priorities, and values as the glue to make Organization-Wide change down and throughout the organization

> **Core Competency #3:** *Create a Strategic Business Design with Watertight Integrity –*
> *"Systemic problems require system-wide solutions."*

3. Develop Leaders Who Can Successfully Lead and implement Changes in the Shared Direction and Strategic Business Design

A. Know your role(s) as a leader
- **leaders**: focus on content and consequences
- **support cadre**: focus on processes and infra-structure coordination

B. Build follow-up structures and processes
- to track, control, adjust and achieve the plan and key success measurements/ results
- to reward, recognize and celebrate progress and results

> **Core Competency #1:** *Develop and Achieve Leadership Excellence –*
> *"Continually increase your range and depth of leadership skills through Leading Strategic Change and Innovation."*

ebsst6.pmd

1420 Monitor Road • San Diego • California • 92110-1545 • (619) 275-6528 • Fax (619) 275-0324

Best Practices Report
International Quality Study

American Quality Foundation (AQF)
and Ernst & Young

Summary of Study

- extensive statistical study
- 945 management practices over 580 organizations (84% response rate)
- in U.S., Japan, Canada, Germany
- automotive, banking, computer, health care industries

Best Practices Lead to High Performance (defined as:)

1. Market performance (perceived quality index)
2. Operations (productivity) performance (value-added per employee)
3. Financial performance (ROA)

Only Three Universally Beneficial Practices

- Only three (3) universally beneficial practices with a significant impact on performance regardless of starting position (rest is a "fit" question of organization – environment – performance)

  1. Strategic Planning/Deployment (Implementation)
  2. Business Process improvement methods (if focused on the customer)
  3. **Continuous broadening of your breadth and depth of leadership and management practices (to make additional gains in performance)**

Background

- Fundamental organizational activities — managing people, processes, technology, and strategy

THREE CORPORATE-WIDE CORE COMPETENCIES

Required of Every Successful Organization in the World

Keyword	Meaning	How to coordinate/ensure it succeeds
#1 **DEVELOP LEADERSHIP**	**Core Competency #1** *"DEVELOP & ACHIEVE LEADERSHIP EXCELLENCE"* Leadership Development System	Employee/Executive Development Board (plus Yearly Leadership Assessment)
#2 **PLANNING CYCLE**	**Core Competency #2** *"BUILD AN INTEGRATED STRATEGIC MANAGEMENT CYCLE"* Overall Strategic Management System	Planning/Strategic Change Steering Committee (plus Annual Strategic Review)
#3 **INTEGRATED CHANGE**	**Core Competency #3** *"CREATE A STRATEGIC BUSINESS DESIGN WITH WATERTIGHT INTEGRITY – TO YOUR VISION"* Integrated architecture of structures, processes, people, and systems to achieve Business Excellence	Strategy Sponsorship and Change Project Teams (plus *Building on Baldrige* Yearly Best Practices Assessment)

"Leading Enterprise-Wide Change"
Means
Leading the Development, Installation and Maintenance of All Three Corporate-Wide Core Competencies
to
Achieve Business Excellence and Superior Results

---

ebsst6.pmd

1420 Monitor Road • San Diego • California • 92110-1545 • (619) 275-6528 • Fax (619) 275-0324

SECTION VII
PLAN-TO-PLAN PROCESS – "Tailored to Your Needs"

BIG THREE ENTERPRISE-WIDE FAILURE ISSUES:

"Guarantee of Failure Up Front"

#1. Analytic and Piecemeal Approach to a System's Problem

- Involving multiple mindsets, frameworks, consultants and fads/silver bullets
- Instead of a *Systems Thinking Approach* and insisting on *Watertight Integrity*

#2. Mainly Focusing on an Economic Alignment of Delivery

- Involving a primary focus on productivity, processes, and bottom-line efficiencies
- Instead of combining this with "attunement" issues below

#3. Mainly Focusing on Cultural Attunement and Involvement with People

- Involving a primary focus on egalitarian, participative, democratic, people processes
- Instead of combining this approach and #2 above (economic alignment)

"Systems Solution":

- An *Enterprise-Wide Systems Thinking Approach* to Business Excellence – with a *Quadruple Bottom Line* measurement system (economics–employees–customers–society)
- *That dramatically increases Superior Results:* (Profits–Growth–Culture–Sustainability)

ebsst7.pmd

1420 Monitor Road • San Diego • California • 92110-1545 • (619) 275-6528 • Fax (619) 275-0324

Take an Architectural (Structural) Approach

Visionary company founders take an architectural approach to building their firms. **They concentrate first on the organization's systems and values, then on products**

The best leaders, charismatic or not, make it a point to develop managers and processes. In their view, the firm is not a vehicle for products or personalities; products are a vehicle for the company.

—Built to Last

5,000 Foot Helicopter View

They work: • *on* their companies

• not *in* their companies

Strategic and Systems Thinking About the Future

"If you do not think about the future,
You cannot have one."

—John Galsworthy

Creating Strategists and Systems Thinkers

Do you have disciplined strategic and
systems thinking in your organization
–or–
just empty rhetoric?

The Winning Formula

"Preparation, discipline and talent,
working within a system,
is the winning playoff formula."

—Michael D. Mitchell
Sporting News

1420 Monitor Road • San Diego • California • 92110-1545 • (619) 275-6528 • Fax (619) 275-0324

ENTERPRISE-WIDE CHANGE

MANY POWERFUL CENTRE APPLICATIONS

(Of the A B C Core Technology)

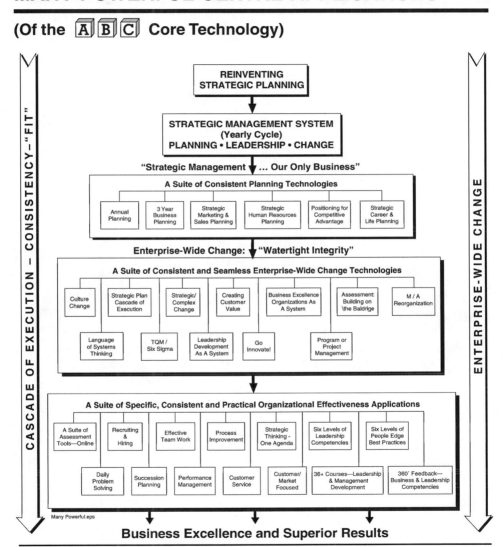

CASCADE OF EXECUTION – CONSISTENCY – "FIT"

ENTERPRISE-WIDE CHANGE

REINVENTING STRATEGIC PLANNING

STRATEGIC MANAGEMENT SYSTEM
(Yearly Cycle)
PLANNING • LEADERSHIP • CHANGE

"Strategic Management ... Our Only Business"

A Suite of Consistent Planning Technologies

| Annual Planning | 3 Year Business Planning | Strategic Marketing & Sales Planning | Strategic Human Resources Planning | Positioning for Competitive Advantage | Strategic Career & Life Planning |

Enterprise-Wide Change: "Watertight Integrity"

A Suite of Consistent and Seamless Enterprise-Wide Change Technologies

| Culture Change | Strategic Plan Cascade of Execution | Strategic/ Complex Change | Creating Customer Value | Business Excellence Organizations As A System | Assessment: Building on \the Baldrige | M / A Reorganization |

| Language of Systems Thinking | TQM / Six Sigma | Leadership Development As A System | Go Innovate! | Program or Project Management |

A Suite of Specific, Consistent and Practical Organizational Effectiveness Applications

| A Suite of Assessment Tools—Online | Recruiting & Hiring | Effective Team Work | Process Improvement | Strategic Thinking - One Agenda | Six Levels of Leadership Competencies | Six Levels of People Edge Best Practices |

| Daily Problem Solving | Succession Planning | Performance Management | Customer Service | Customer/ Market Focused | 36+ Courses—Leadership & Management Development | 360˚ Feedback— Business & Leadership Competencies |

Many Powerful.eps

Business Excellence and Superior Results

All based on one holistic and seamless construct: The Systems Thinking Approach℠

ebsst7.pmd

1420 Monitor Road • San Diego • California • 92110-1545 • (619) 275-6528 • Fax (619) 275-0324

THE PLAYERS OF ENTERPRISE-WIDE CHANGE

1420 Monitor Road • San Diego • California • 92110-1545 • (619) 275-6528 • Fax (619) 275-0324

THE PLAYERS OF ENTERPRISE-WIDE CHANGE

1. **Change Leaders/Champions:**

   - The individual or group that recognizes that change is needed and accepts responsibility for initiating the required change. Must include CEO and senior management.

2. **Change Consultants/Facilitators:**

   - The individual or group that agrees with the need for change and accepts responsibility for facilitating the required change. Must be SMEs (Subject Matter Experts) on the processes and structures of change.

3. **Change Implementers (All Management and All Employees):**

   - The individuals or groups that understand and accept the need for change and actually implement the desired change within their daily work and behaviors.

(Always includes the Change Leaders/Consultants because they must "walk the talk")

4. **Program Management Office: Enterprise-Wide Change:**

   - Joint internal and external experts (executive and consultant) in Content, Process, Structural Knowledge, and Skills of successful Enterprise-Wide change efforts.

   - It requires both an executive and a consultant who are well-respected and have high credibility, reporting directly to the CEO. They must have no other day-to-day responsibilities except the Enterprise-Wide Change effort (e.g., the same way that Boeing builds aircraft to create future business).

   - Be sure to provide them, at minimum, with support staff, a financial analyst, space, and a budget.

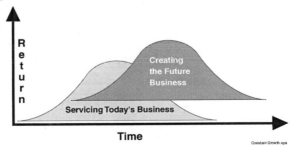

ebsst7.pmd

1420 Monitor Road • San Diego • California • 92110-1545 • (619) 275-6528 • Fax (619) 275-0324

STRATEGIC CHANGE LEADERSHIP STEERING COMMITTEE

CRITERIA FOR THE CORE CHANGE TEAM SELECTION

Organization-Wide vs. Narrow Perspective?

- Each core Strategic Change Leadership Steering Committee team participant must be willing to have an Enterprise-Wide perspective and orientation in order to be on the team. Status quo, narrow perspectives and interests, or *representing only parts of the organization* must be left *at the door* in order for Enterprise-Wide Change to be successful.

- The Strategic Change Leadership Steering Committee is not a collection of special interest groups coming together but individuals willing to look at the "Gestalt" or whole organization as it interacts both in its dynamic environment and inner workings as well.

- An openness to future change is a key requirement for success, as is a focus on the customer and the environment.

- However, their functional perspective is also appropriate...in order to implement the Enterprise-Wide Change through their annual department, and individual action plans.

#1 Strategic Change Leadership Steering Committee Composition – People With:
- A fundamental understanding of the strategic direction
- Ownership and commitment — CEO and senior level/middle management
- Data reality — key players
- Stakeholders — key to broad perspective
- An ability to help with implementation — key players
- A staff support team (internal/external)
- Leader preference and comfort

#2 Numbers Vs. Group Dynamics Reasonableness
A. 6-8 people = best size for group dynamics/team building
B. 10-15 people = okay size (2-3 subgroups)
C. 16+ people = a "mess" — crowd control becomes the issue

#3 Involvement of Others Through Parallel Process/Participation Schemes
- Through whole system/large-scale meetings and events
- Through data collection and feedback
- Through involvement in business/annual department action planning
- Through asking their opinions/reactions to proposed actions/directions/changes

ebsst7.pmd

1420 Monitor Road • San Diego • California • 92110-1545 • (619) 275-6528 • Fax (619) 275-0324

"STAFF SUPPORT TEAM"

Enterprise-Wide Change

List Staff Support Team Names:

Support Cadre	Typical Tasks	Name
1. Planning	• Enterprise-Wide Change Planning • Business Unit Change Planning • Current State Assessment/ Research	
2. **Finance**	• Key Success Measure Coordinator • Budgeting • Current State Assessment/ Economics	
3. **Human Resources**	• Performance/Rewards Management • Training and Development	
4. **Communications**	• Updates After Each Meeting • Print Final Game Plan • Communication Plan	
5. **Administrative Assistant**	• Logistics/Follow-up • Laptop Minutes/Document Revisions • Drafts Enterprise-Wide Change Game Plan	
6a. **Program Management Office:** Internal Coordinator coordinates or does 1-6	**Minimum List** • Parallel Process/Participative Scheme • Internal Facilitator • Coordinates Entire Enterprise-Wide Process • Facilitates/Supports the Strategic Change Leadership Committee	
6b. **External Consultant** (Systems Consultant) Program Management Office	• Facilitate Innovative Change Project Teams • Develops Internal Coordinator • Devil's Advocate/Tough Choices • Advisor on all Enterprise-Wide Change • Subject Matter Experts (SME)	

ebsst7.pmd

SST Executive Briefing. All Rights reserved.

1420 Monitor Road • San Diego • California • 92110-1545 • (619) 275-6528 • Fax (619) 275-0324

THE EXTERNAL CONSULTANT ROLE

Program Management Leadership

1. Jointly leads the day-to-day Enterprise-Wide Change structures and processes along with the internal executive leader.

   • To coordinate integration across multiple projects and processes.

   • Ensuring innovative Best Practices Results for each project within the overall process.

   • Gaining the Superior Results and ROI requirements of each Enterprise-Wide Change process.

2. Acts as a "devil's advocate" by posing frank questions on:

   • following the core values in the Enterprise-Wide Change process.

   • pushing for concrete decisions, directions, and priorities.

   • helping the CEO do what needs to be done, based on what the CEO said they want to achieve in Enterprise-Wide Change.

   • challenging the CEO and key people about the issues they are backing away from; helping them make the hard decisions.

   • moving from Vision to Reality.

3. Constantly crafts and facilitates the Enterprise-Wide Change process jointly with the internal executive, but lets the CEO determine the direction of the changes and their future.

4. Brings mastery-levels expertise—content (business and people) teacher-coach, and process facilitation – with objectivity.

5. Assists your internal staff support team in:

   • being a teacher to line managers/executives.

   • assisting the CEO and executives to regularly communicate with the rest of the organization about the Enterprise-Wide Change.

6. Assists you in developing an overall **Leadership Development System (Corporate-Wide Core Competency #1)** tied to your Strategic Direction.

7. Facilitates your Strategic Management process to ensure that you build your first **Strategic Management Yearly Cycle (Corporate-Wide Core Competency #2).**

8. Assists you in implementing the results of the Business Excellence Assessment (Building on Baldrige – Best Practices) to ensure **"Watertight Integrity" to your Vision, Values, and Positioning (Corporate-Wide Core Competency #3).**

1420 Monitor Road • San Diego • California • 92110-1545 • (619) 275-6528 • Fax (619) 275-0324

THE EXTERNAL CONSULTANT ROLE

Program Management Leadership *(continued)*

Consultant Skills in Enterprise-Wide Change:

Seven Requirements

1. A strong business, economic, and industry sector orientation

2. Extensive knowledge and skills in Enterprise-Wide change and Systems Thinking

3. Strong expertise in strategic planning and project management

4. An excellent sense of overall organization fit, functioning, and organization design (for Watertight Integrity)

5. Understanding and skills in human behavior and group/organizational dynamics and facilitation

6. In-depth skills in the consulting process, executive coaching, and meetings management

7. Strong internal sense of self, ego-less , and self-esteem coupled with humility and courage

ebsst7.pmd

1420 Monitor Road • San Diego • California • 92110-1545 • (619) 275-6528 • Fax (619) 275-0324

TAILORED TO YOUR NEEDS – GAP ANALYSIS

Enterprise-Wide Change: The Systems Thinking Approach^{SM}

Based on your understanding of the Systems Thinking Approach^{SM} to Enterprise-Wide change, list the importance of the following new initiatives for achieving Business Excellence and Superior Results for your organization.
H = High - Start within the next 6 months • **M = Moderate** - Start within the next 12 months
L = Low - Start within the next 1 - 3 years • **N/A** = Not needed/no further work needed by your organization.

IMPORTANCE
(H - M - L - N/A)

NEW INITIATIVES - MANY POWERFUL CENTRE APPLICATIONS

1. New Systems Thinking language becomes a key part of our culture.
2. Develop Strategic Thinkers among our collective management on a daily basis.
3. Develop Strategic Thinkers among all employees on a daily basis.
4. Develop a common model (paradigm/framework/mental map) to use for your "Organization as a System".
5. Conduct an Enterprise-Wide Business Excellence Assessment ("Building on the Baldrige" – Best Practices).
6. Conduct a **"one-agenda" Systems Thinking Day** on a critical issue. List: _____
7. Develop and implement a Strategic Plan using the Strategic Thinking Approach^{SM}
8. Develop your own unique Strategic Management System and Yearly Cycle.
9. Install a full Enterprise-Wide Change effort.
10. Develop and implement a 3-year Business Plan for Line Units/Divisions/LOBs/SBUs.
11. Develop and implement a 3-year People Plan for the Enterprise (Strategic HR Plan)
12. Develop and implement a 3-year Strategic Marketing and Sales plan.
13. Clarify your unique Positioning in the marketplace vs. the Competition in the eyes of the customer to create Customer Value.
14. Create a System of Leadership Development for the collective management team.
15. Create a System of Succession Planning for Key Jobs/Roles (include executives).
16. Create a culture change to a positive work environment and a High Performance Organization.
17. Create Innovation as a core value and set of skills throughout the organization.
18. Create a Knowledge Management System and a Learning Organization.
19. Enhance Business Excellence (effectiveness and efficiency) on a day-to-day operational level.
20. Reorganize to create more simplicity, flexibility, and responsiveness to changes in the marketplace.

ENGINEER SUCCESS UP FRONT

The Bottom Line on "How to Begin"

I. Establish the following:

✔ 1.   Install the Executive Team as the Strategic Change Leadership Steering Committee with the necessary sub-structures (see "menu").

✔ 2.   Set up and train on "Internal Support Cadre" with the knowledge and skills to accomplish our new initiatives and desired outcomes.

✔ 3.   Establish a Program Management Office with joint leaders – a creditable internal executive and outside consultant.

✔ 4.   Train your collective management team to acquire the knowledge and skills to accomplish our desired outcomes – see attached multi-year cultural change efforts.

✔ 5.   Conduct the needed organizational/marketplace assessments vs. Proven Best Practices to ensure that we have a solid base of reality from which to begin.

✔ 6.   Design a rollout, communications, development, and sustained involvement process for "buy-in" and "stay-in" to the desired outcomes.

✔ 7.   Redesign performance, incentive, and recognition programs to support these efforts.

✔ 8.   Develop an overall 1-3 year Enterprise-Wide Change "Game Plan".

✔ 9.   Develop a yearly comprehensive map of Implementation for the next 12 months.

✔ 10.   Develop a budget and resources to support your Game Plan along with some ROI targets.

MULTIYEAR CULTURAL CHANGE EFFORT

"DRIP-DRIP" JOINT DEVELOPMENTAL EXPERIENCES

Concept: Take the entire Senior Management Collective Leadership Team (up to 30-40 people max.) through an intense 2-5 day training and development experience **together 1-2 times per year.**

Then:

Goal: Use it to develop, focus the attention, action plan and kick off of the entire organization's approach to one of a number of key topics of cultural change.

Suggested Sequence/Flow: (Put H-M-L on your priorities)

I.   Initial Topics (in a tailored order)

_____ 1. Strategic and Systems Thinking

_____ 2. Reinventing Strategic Management

_____ 3. Leading Enterprise-Wide Change

_____ 4. Strategic Leadership Development

_____ 5. Conflict Management—Ethical Persuasion

_____ 6. Coaching for Commitment

_____ 7. Group Facilitation (and Participative Decision Making) for Leaders

_____ 8. Innovation and Creativity

II. Additional Key Topics in Cultural Change (in no order)

_____ 1. Creating the People Edge

_____ 2. Creating Customer Value

_____ 3. Blowing Out Bureaucracy

_____ 4. Organization and Process Redesign

_____ 5. Learning and the Learning Organization

_____ 6. Effective Team Building (Teams Everywhere)

_____ 7. Negotiating—Win-Win

_____ 8. Train-the-Trainer for Managers

_____ 9. Personal and Supervisory Transition Management

_____ 10. Excellence in Customer Service

1420 Monitor Road • San Diego • California • 92110-1545 • (619) 275-6528 • Fax (619) 275-0324

HOW TO MAKE THE PEOPLE IN THE ORGANIZATION UNDERSTAND AND USE SYSTEMS THINKING

Unless the massive frontal approach works, use bite size practical tools/topics:

1. Teach the Systems Questions one at a time, i.e., #1 first – What is our goal?

2. Use/teach the "Systems Solutions" model and use it in a practical, helpful way (not the old "problem solving" model.

3. Use/teach the ABCDE Systems Model to describe the change project (or the Strategic Planning project.)

4. Work with project teams to learn the ABC's, the 10 Questions, and apply them to their project.

5. Help people understand the "Rollercoaster of Change", just before it's needed.

6. Use the "Six Natural Rings of Reality" model to teach the "7 Levels of Living Systems" in a practical, common sense manner. Use this as your Leverage Point for initiating change.

7. Put the Systems Thinking Approach^{SM} in all your Management Development programs – integrate the programs better as one system using System Thinking Structures.

8. Share the Employee Handbooks #1 and #2 and Job Aid (Trifold) with all employees as they are very simple and useful to apply on a daily basis.

9. Introduce one or two of the "Inner Workings" in the 12 Systems Characteristics (such as entropy) and show/use it in a practical way. Set up a 52-week "Drip", "Bite-sized" Learning System.

10. Have executives do personal Strategic Life Planning as a way to learn Systems Thinking and the A-B-C-D-E Model.

11. Provide one-on-one coaching for the CEO/key Senior Executives and show them how Systems Thinking helps with their issues/problems in a practical way.

12. Teach the Strategic and Systems Thinking Approach (Four Key Concepts) in workshops for all management and employees from the top down (1 - 3 day programs).

13. Have each executive read **"The Managers Pocket Guide to Systems Thinking and Learning"** as pre-work to any training. After the training, have them read **"Enterprise-Wide Change: The Systems Thinking Approach to Superior Results"**.

14. Have each executive develop an "Individual Leadership Plan" on three ways they can use Systems Thinking. Set regular follow-up team sessions on the status and results accomplished.

ebsst7.pmd

1420 Monitor Road • San Diego • California • 92110-1545 • (619) 275-6528 • Fax (619) 275-0324

The Natural Laws of All Living Systems

The Goal (in Whatever We Do)

"Clarify and Simplify – Clarify and Simplify – Clarify and Simplify"

Management's Ultimate Challenge

"Search for the simplicity on the far side of complexity"

A Output

FUTURE

E Environment

D Throughput

"THE SYSTEM"

B Feedback

Feedback Loop

C Input

TODAY

Why Thinking Matters

The way you think creates the results you get.

The most powerful way to improve the quality of your results is to improve the way you think.

Why Thinking Matters

How you think...
is how you act...
is how you are.

ebsst7.pmd

1420 Monitor Road • San Diego • California • 92110-1545 • (619) 275-6528 • Fax (619) 275-0324

A STRATEGIC MANAGEMENT SYSTEM

(is the #2 Core Competency of Every Organization)

Time Management and Organization Effectiveness

A Systems Thinking Approach℠ & Commitment

to a

Strategic Management System, and Cycle
(Planning, Leadership and Change)

is the **ultimate**

- Time Management
- Team Building
- Conflict Resolution
- Organizational Effectiveness and
- Executive Development tool

for

an entire organization.

THE RESULT: Business Excellence and Superior Results!

There is nothing else even close!
(All the rest are a series of well-meaning, piecemeal efforts)

ebsst7.pmd

1420 Monitor Road • San Diego • California • 92110-1545 • (619) 275-6528 • Fax (619) 275-0324

YOUR THOUGHTS AND YOUR DESTINY

"Keep your Thoughts positive because your thoughts become your words;

Keep your words positive because your words become your behavior;

Keep your behavior positive because your behaviors become your habits;

Keep your habits positive because your habits become your values;

Keep your values positive because your values become your Destiny."

1420 Monitor Road • San Diego • California • 92110-1545 • (619) 275-6528 • Fax (619) 275-0324